CREATS, CRAILS AND CAVERN CALES.

For Jill and Ivan Carter-Becker, Sharon and Thomas Spain
and all who appreciate the legendary beauty of Teesdale.

Written and Designed by Hugh Becker.
Illustrated by Mark Spain.
Barnard Castle, County Durham.
MCMXCV.

First Softback Edition
sponsored by

CARLSBERG-TETLEY

CONTENTS:

*All the Trails are sketched for guidance only and are not intended to be exact representations of Public Rights of Way. Please always check your route at the time and follow signs and markers. Ordnance Survey Landranger 92 (1:50,000) and Outdoor Leisure 31 (1:25,000) will be useful.

THE BROWNLOW ARMS,
CALDWELL

3

A List of Illustrated Plates:

THE FORESTERS,
MIDDLETON-IN-TEESDALE

5

INTRODUCTION

Some time ago, I received a request to take an emergency supply of beer to the Strathmore Arms at Holwick, a building steeped in history and sometimes described as "the most isolated tavern in all England". A blizzard was forecast for later that evening and the landlord feared that he might be cut off for a day or two.

On my way there, close to the Inn, I passed an old man slowly walking along beside the single track road. The wind was fierce and chill. I stopped and offered him a lift. He was clearly cold, inadequately, you might even have thought rather quaintly dressed, and he seemed to me to be somewhat dazed, a little uncertain of quite where he was and even of where he was going to.

I took him into the bar, sat him in front of the welcoming fire with a brandy and asked him if he was hungry; he nodded and, while his food was prepared, began to speak and to tell me tales of times past and of legendary events that occurred in Teesdale. His knowledge seemed to be extraordinary and I sat entranced as he painted vivid pictures with his words.

Whilst he spoke, he sketched in pencil on the back of some old rolls of paper which he had stuffed in a worn leather pouch. He drew, as quickly as his rough gnarled hand would allow, miniature scenes to illustrate his tales. I had no sense of the passing time, but later, it seemed only moments, the old man rose abruptly as if summoned by the calling of some far away voice and promptly took his leave.

I tried to ask him where he would go in the storm, where he would sleep. He did not answer, save to thank me for the food and for listening to his tales.

The landlord placed his hand lightly upon my shoulder as he collected the empty plate and asked, "Did you enjoy your meal? That brandy must have made you sleepy. You have been sitting here beside the fire, muttering to yourself and scribbling away for ages."

I did not dare ask him or anyone else crowded around the fire that night whether they had seen the old man or heard his tales. I knew instinctively that they would not have done. I slipped his sketches into my pocket and left to drive home even as the heavy snow began to blanket the surrounding hills. Outside the Inn I could see no tracks nor find any trace of the old man at all.

You may imagine my wonder and surprise when, upon my return, I discovered that the rolled up scraps of paper were in fact maps of the old circular pathways in the Dale. The paper had already begun to disintegrate and I sat down immediately to record the tales and trails as faithfully as I could, and you may read the stories, walk the trails and judge them for yourselves. I may be guilty of some small inaccuracies but they remain, to this day, as clear in my memory as they were on that stormy winter's evening when the old man sat at the fireside with me and with me alone.

THE STRATHMORE ARMS,
HOLWICK

7

A TAVERN TALE TOUR OF
TEESDALE

the FORESTERS
At middleton.

the KING'S HEAD
At middleton.

the BRIDGE inn
At middleton.

the strathmore ARMS
At holwick

the BLAC
At

the STAG'S HEAD INN
AT BUTTERKNOWLE.

the RABY MOOR INN
AT BURNTHOUSES

the OLD WELL INN
AT BARNARD CASTLE.

the BRIDGE inn
AT WHORLTON.

ith's ARMS
leton

the OAK TREE inn
AT HUTTON MAGNA.

the BROWNLOW ARMS
AT CALDWELL.

Che Crout's Cale

azing in a sunlit dappled stream, invisible against the mosaic pebbled bed, brown trout only move to feed on nymphs or hatched flies skating temptingly on the surface film; momentary explosive dashes to sink quietly to wait again and again.

As newly hatched fry, shoaling in the warm still shallows and rock pools which abound by the river's margins, the tales are told of how man loves to pit his wits against the sharp eyes of the fish and to make artificial flies with which to catch the unwary on hook and line.

In the olden days, when the ruined walls of Crossthwaite village still stood gaunt and ragged in the river meadows, two such men used to delight in fishing together for company in the fast flowing waters of the river. Their favourite shaded pool lay a little upstream from the bridge which now carries the new road into Middleton, hard by the Bridge Inn tavern.

They were two very different men; the one generous, attuned to nature, the other selfish aware only of his own desires but, as is often the way of men, their differences created a common bond of friendship between them.

The good man fished for pleasure, he used only a simple hook on which he had not raised a barb so that when he caught a young fish, he might release it gently back into the peaty water unharmed. He understood the balance which Nature demands of all its creatures, studying, sketching and recording the detail and the beauty of that which surrounded him. He tied his trout flies with such dexterity and grace that he rarely fished without success.

His companion, however, was impatient with all such matters. He desired quite simply to catch as many fish as he could and to carry them all home regardless of their size or number. Fortunately for the river trout, his impatience extended to the tying of his flies and all but the most naive knew to avoid his ugly and exaggerated lures, some even made crude sport with him, swirling close to or even flicking his horsehair line with their tails to drive the hapless angler into a frenzy of rage and despair.

10

One such day, his temper not at all improved by the sight of his companion cheerfully returning what appeared to be an endless succession of freely taking trout back into the river, he asked if he might try one of his friend's cunningly tied patterns for a change. The good humoured man readily agreed and the greedy man soon filled his wicker basket to overflowing.

The oldest brown trout in the river, sometimes glimpsed but never caught, had seen these events unfold and was alarmed. The broad tail flexed and the good man caught his breath as he saw a dark shadow glide from behind a rock, rising to pluck his fly from the stream.

Overjoyed, the good man played the much prized fish and drew it gently over his outstretched landing net. "Good Man", said the fish, "I have sacrificed myself to ask that you never again shall give your companion one of your cunningly contrived baits". Astonished, the good man understood the noble trout's request and, as one sportsman acknowledging another, gently slipped the unharmed fish back into the cool, reviving flow.

That evening, as the sun sank low over Cross Fell, the good man, sitting at his kitchen table, chuckling with mirth, began to tie a batch of crude and ugly lures with which to satisfy his impatient friend's demands and, strange to say, from that day on, try as he might, the greedy man never caught another trout in the waters of the River Tees.

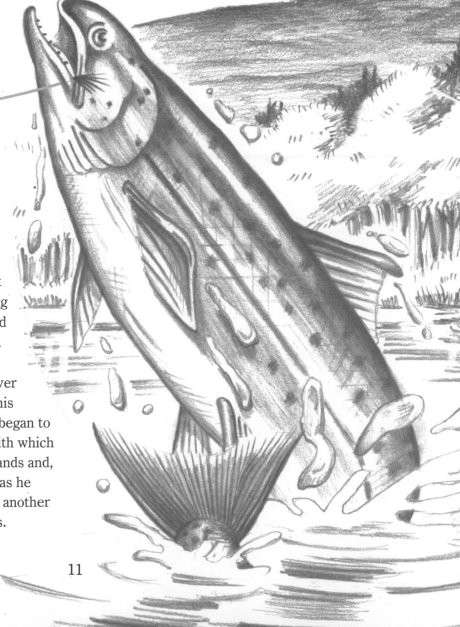

11

the trout's travels.

(6 miles, 10 kilometers, easy walking, with variations possible.)

The Bridge Inn is early nineteenth century and, therefore, a rough contemporary of the road bridge over the River Tees, completed successfully after an initial disaster (see page 56), and our walk commences by turning southwards, down the hill from the Bridge Inn and over the said bridge [1], with the sheep market on your right.

If, as you cross the river, you cast your eye upwards to the skyline in front of you, you will see the silhouette of Kirkcarrion, a mystical place, reputedly the burial site of Caryn, an Iron Age Prince of the Brigantes, the indigenous tribe who fought the Roman Legions in 80A.D. (see page 44). The massive funereal cairn was dismantled in 1804, revealing a cinerary urn, since lost. The stones from the cairn were reused to build enclosure walls on Crossthwaite Fell. Around the turn of the last century, this spot overlooked Middleton's own, long abandoned, nine hole golf course, which must have offered Edwardian golfers a testing round.

The Brigantes, meaning 'upland people', were Celtic speaking and may have named the Tees from their word 'Tes', similar to the Welsh word for heat and sunshine, as a boiling, sparkling river. The Tees Valley and adjacent Stainmore Pass represented two key Trans-Pennine routes for the passage of commerce and the conduct of war.

Turning right, you enter the river meadows where once stood the village of Crossthwaite [2], like so many, abandoned due to fighting with Scottish border raiders or the Normans, maybe decimated by plague, such as the Black Death of 1351, a Bubonic Plague spread by the fleas carried on Black Rats, or simply a victim of famine or other causes. The stone has been 'robbed' for other walls and buildings and no trace remains today.

The dark cliff faces to your left [3], are the Whin-Sill quarries, opened around 1868, by Ord and Maddison. The exceptionally hard quartz-dolerite, dating from two hundred and ninety million years ago, was worked for paving slabs and crushed for road stone, the machinery was driven by water impounded in fell ponds high above the workings. The quarry, now idle, but employing two hundred and thirty one men in 1920, shipped its products to market by the railway, which was intended to continue through to Alston. The extension was surveyed in 1869 but never financed, Middleton Station with its gardens and miniature waterfall remained the main line terminus, although a private light railway was built to service all the quarries including Park End.

As your path approaches a meander in the river bed, you will see Park End Wood [4] on your left. This is the last vestige of the Forest of Teesdale, which covered thousands of acres, mainly on the northern side of the Tees. The deciduous woodland was comprised largely of Juniper, Alder, Hazel, Elm, Oak and Birch and the dense cover provided an excellent habitat for wolves, bears, boar and wild cats, as well as deer and wild cattle. Small wonder that these forests were highly regarded for hunting, but inevitably, bit by bit, climatic change and the demands of stock grazing saw them cleared to become pasture.

Now that you are walking close to the river's edge, you may see a fish rise to take a fly from the surface. In 1983, the main river was subjected to a devastating pollution from a spill of Flux oil at the Hargreaves Quarry above High Force (see page 24). Thousands of fish, Salmon, Sea Trout, Grayling and Brown Trout were killed in the upper reaches and a substantial number of coarse fish died in the lower reaches. The entire food chain was disrupted and the river is only just recovering fully, some twelve years after the incident. Many people consider that the large scale re-stocking programme may have corrupted the genetic integrity of the native fish stocks and the full effects remain to be seen in time (see page 48).

12

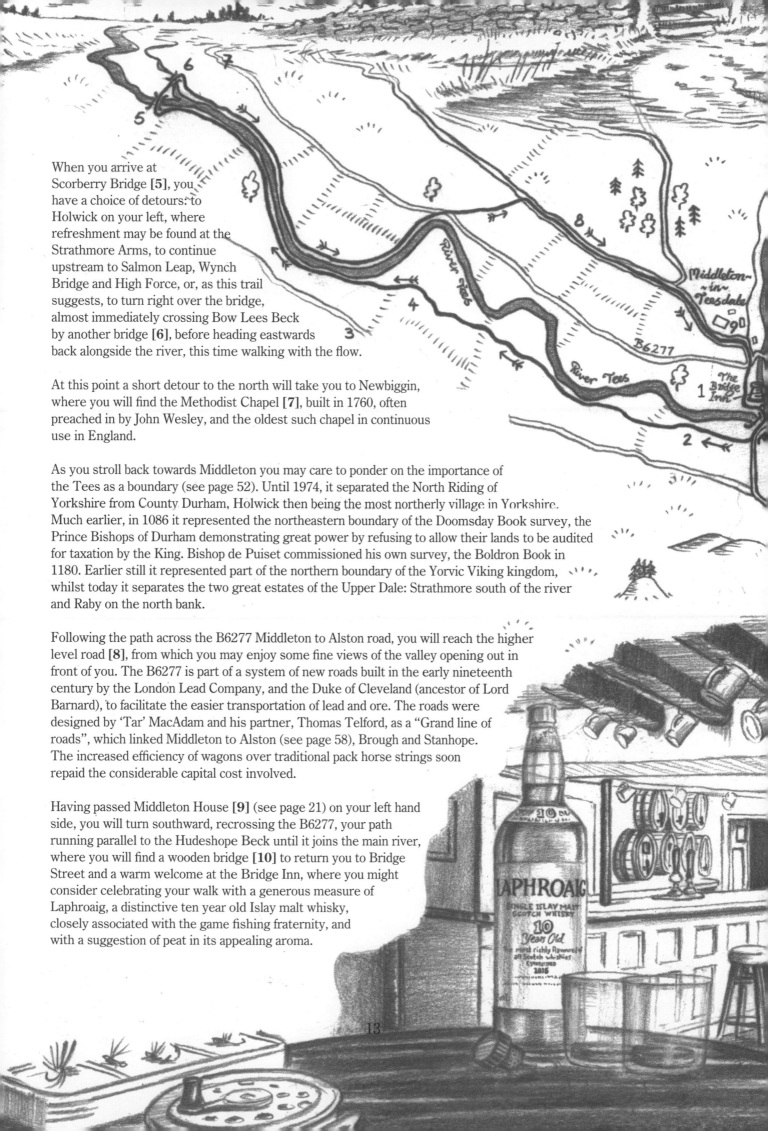

When you arrive at Scorberry Bridge [5], you have a choice of detours: to Holwick on your left, where refreshment may be found at the Strathmore Arms, to continue upstream to Salmon Leap, Wynch Bridge and High Force, or, as this trail suggests, to turn right over the bridge, almost immediately crossing Bow Lees Beck by another bridge [6], before heading eastwards back alongside the river, this time walking with the flow.

At this point a short detour to the north will take you to Newbiggin, where you will find the Methodist Chapel [7], built in 1760, often preached in by John Wesley, and the oldest such chapel in continuous use in England.

As you stroll back towards Middleton you may care to ponder on the importance of the Tees as a boundary (see page 52). Until 1974, it separated the North Riding of Yorkshire from County Durham, Holwick then being the most northerly village in Yorkshire. Much earlier, in 1086 it represented the northeastern boundary of the Doomsday Book survey, the Prince Bishops of Durham demonstrating great power by refusing to allow their lands to be audited for taxation by the King. Bishop de Puiset commissioned his own survey, the Boldron Book in 1180. Earlier still it represented part of the northern boundary of the Yorvic Viking kingdom, whilst today it separates the two great estates of the Upper Dale: Strathmore south of the river and Raby on the north bank.

Following the path across the B6277 Middleton to Alston road, you will reach the higher level road [8], from which you may enjoy some fine views of the valley opening out in front of you. The B6277 is part of a system of new roads built in the early nineteenth century by the London Lead Company, and the Duke of Cleveland (ancestor of Lord Barnard), to facilitate the easier transportation of lead and ore. The roads were designed by 'Tar' MacAdam and his partner, Thomas Telford, as a "Grand line of roads", which linked Middleton to Alston (see page 58), Brough and Stanhope. The increased efficiency of wagons over traditional pack horse strings soon repaid the considerable capital cost involved.

Having passed Middleton House [9] (see page 21) on your left hand side, you will turn southward, recrossing the B6277, your path running parallel to the Hudeshope Beck until it joins the main river, where you will find a wooden bridge [10] to return you to Bridge Street and a warm welcome at the Bridge Inn, where you might consider celebrating your walk with a generous measure of Laphroaig, a distinctive ten year old Islay malt whisky, closely associated with the game fishing fraternity, and with a suggestion of peat in its appealing aroma.

13

THE FARM DOG'S TALE

In the days before books were widely available, when television had yet to be invented, symbols and pictures were of great importance, and none more so than the traditional, pictorial tavern signs which hung above many an innkeeper's door, promising good ale, food, company and a cheap bed for the weary traveller. Where there was no picture painted, the common symbol for the tavern was a bush.

One winter evening, the harsh blizzard abating momentarily, a finely cloaked horseman stumbled through the drifting snow into the cobbled yard of farm steading, which stood close by Middleton, on the southern bank of the River Tees, a short way downstream from the stepping stone crossing. The stranger entered the simple kitchen and bade the Farmer's wife to bring him a bowl of broth and to find shelter and forage for his tired mount.

With his short sword, loosed from its elaborate scabbard and laid ready upon the rough wooden table before him, the stranger had barely begun his meal when the Farmer returned from feeding and sheltering his flock as best he could, his two dogs close to his heels.

The Farmer's wife, not knowing whether the silent nobleman was friend or foe and fearful that her husband's quick temper might provoke their uninvited guest to raise his bright sword against them both, motioned the farmer to follow her straightway into the bare hallway.

In low tones the Farmer questioned his wife concerning the nature and disposition of the noble lord.

14

Whilst she protested her ignorance, the two dogs padded softly past the table, glancing briefly at the fierce face of the diner.

"It is the King!" growled one hound softly to the other; "I have seen his likeness painted above a tavern in the village; the one which stands close by the corn mill. Neither our master nor our mistress have recognized Him and thereby lies much danger for this house." Her companion nodded, rising from the warm fireplace where he had just settled to guard the door to the hallway.

The Farmer, still questioning his wife, was left speechless as both dogs took hold of his well worn cloak and pulled him towards the outer door, the bitch deftly raising the crude iron latch with her soft muzzle.

Out into the clear and frosty moonlit night went the strange trio, the bitch loping before making a track through the drifted snow, with the dog by his master's side, still holding the ragged hem of his cloak in his powerful jaws. The procession halted beneath the sign hanging above the King's Head Tavern, and soon the Farmer's eye caught sight of the face which stared down at him with regal gaze.

Straight way the Farmer hurried home as the chill wind began to drive the first flurrying flakes of the renewing storm across the valley. He entered the kitchen and fell on bended knee before the seated stranger saying; "Sire, my humble household is yours to command as you will."

The King's grip upon his sword relaxed. "Gentle swain" quoth he, "These are troubled times in which We reign. Thy loyalty and the hospitality of thine house will be rewarded once We are reunited with Our hunting party, from whose company this storm hath so rudely parted Us."

The following morning, the scattered retinue having been reassembled, the King kept his word and decreed that the Farmer and his wife should be granted title to the farm and all the lands thereto attached. Thenceforward, neither the Farmer nor his wife scolded their dogs again, nor did either mutter curses when the royal hunting horns rang out from the Forest of Teesdale, causing the far hills to echo with their strident clamour.

The FARM DOG'S STROLL.

(3 miles, 4.5 kilometers, easy walking.)

Stone arches abound in the architecture of Middleton. The two which led down to the stables behind the King's Head and the Foresters are typical and reflect the stone vaulted entrance portals to many lead mines which were often proudly embellished with similarly skilled masonry and graced with inscribed keystones.

The present King's Head stands within the oldest parts of Middleton; certainly a Viking village and possibly much older. The high ground on either side of the Hudeshope Beck was chosen by early settlers because it was clear of the devastating floods which could occur after a snow melt or a storm on the fells, creating the fast moving wall of water known as the 'Tees Roll' (see page 48). The great flood of 1771 is reputed to have raised the river level twenty five feet above its previously recorded flood level.

Progress southwards through the broad Market Place, still used by local farmers until the Public Health Act of 1924 moved live animal markets out of town centres, and thence down Bridge Street to turn left [1] just before the bridge itself. You will pass the Bainbridge Memorial Fountain [2], erected like its counterpart at Nenthead, in recognition of the respect and esteem in which this particular retiring Supervisor of the London Lead Company was held by the populace. In 1832, the Company employed ninety percent of the town's work force.

The London Lead Company, sometimes referred to as the Quaker Company, formed in 1692 under a royal charter of William and Mary, transformed Middleton from a village in 1760 to a thriving industrial town, with dire consequences on its liquidation in 1905. Not only did it introduce the first five day working week in England, create the first co-operative store, the Teesdale Workingman's Corn Association, and introduce a system of credit payments to miners, the Ready Money Shop, but, commencing in 1815, it also built much of the town [3] and its first school. Strangely, the Company did not build a Quaker church in Middleton.

The path downstream, the beginning of the forty mile Teesdale Way Walk to Tees Mouth and the sea, passes a gauging station [4]. This exists to monitor the river flow, measured in cumecs, or cubic meters per second. All the reservoirs of Teesdale, and particularly Cow Green with nine thousand million gallons impounded, exist to serve the towns and industries in the lower part of the catchment. The system is also linked by tunnel and pumping station to the River Wear at Stanhope and thence to the Tyne at Riding Mill, allowing water to be transferred from Kielder Water, with a capacity of forty four billion gallons, in time of drought or emergency.

Just upstream from Step Ends Farm on the southern bank is the site of the old stepping stone crossing [5], used before the river was spanned by the County Bridge in 1811 (see page 56); and to your left stood the Medieval Town Fields. In order to preclude anyone other than the Lord of the Manor amassing a significant land holding, individual strips or furlongs were allocated annually by lot to families who were duty bound to farm the whole field in a communal manner, paying 'tithes', literally the payment of one tenth of all produce, or its equivalent value in labour, to the Lord of the Manor. These agricultural units, known as oxgangs or bovates, represented the area which one ox could plough and harrow each season. The size of each strip would depend on the soil quality and gradient of the land.

In the late seventeenth century the pattern of small arable units producing grain changed to larger pastures supplying the growing market for meat created by the fast expanding and hungry labour force on the Durham Coal-fields, which lay to the east of the County (see pages 52 and 53).

Leaving the waterside and turning northwards [6], you will cross the B6282 Middleton to Barnard Castle road, turnpiked to generate toll revenue in 1792 as part of the important coal road to Woodland and the opencast coal pits some ten miles to the east. Gas Works Lane [7] is a throw back from the time when Middleton enjoyed a

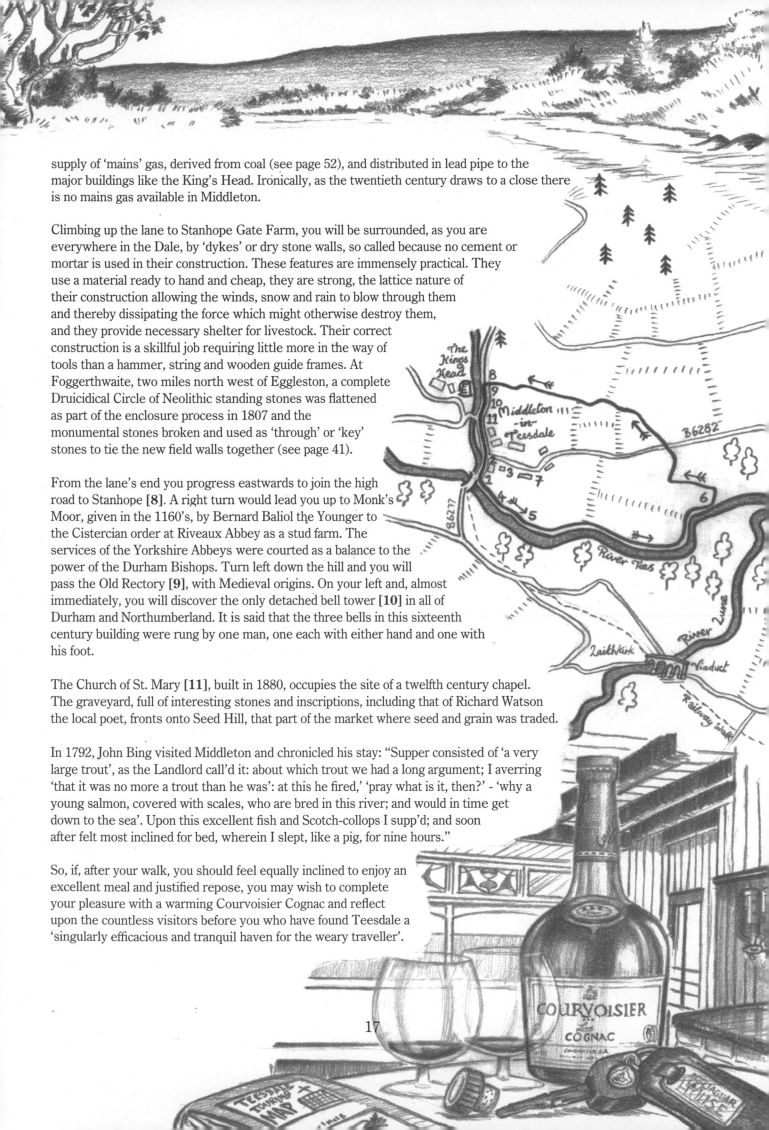

supply of 'mains' gas, derived from coal (see page 52), and distributed in lead pipe to the major buildings like the King's Head. Ironically, as the twentieth century draws to a close there is no mains gas available in Middleton.

Climbing up the lane to Stanhope Gate Farm, you will be surrounded, as you are everywhere in the Dale, by 'dykes' or dry stone walls, so called because no cement or mortar is used in their construction. These features are immensely practical. They use a material ready to hand and cheap, they are strong, the lattice nature of their construction allowing the winds, snow and rain to blow through them and thereby dissipating the force which might otherwise destroy them, and they provide necessary shelter for livestock. Their correct construction is a skillful job requiring little more in the way of tools than a hammer, string and wooden guide frames. At Foggerthwaite, two miles north west of Eggleston, a complete Druicidical Circle of Neolithic standing stones was flattened as part of the enclosure process in 1807 and the monumental stones broken and used as 'through' or 'key' stones to tie the new field walls together (see page 41).

From the lane's end you progress eastwards to join the high road to Stanhope [8]. A right turn would lead you up to Monk's Moor, given in the 1160's, by Bernard Baliol the Younger to the Cistercian order at Riveaux Abbey as a stud farm. The services of the Yorkshire Abbeys were courted as a balance to the power of the Durham Bishops. Turn left down the hill and you will pass the Old Rectory [9], with Medieval origins. On your left and, almost immediately, you will discover the only detached bell tower [10] in all of Durham and Northumberland. It is said that the three bells in this sixteenth century building were rung by one man, one each with either hand and one with his foot.

The Church of St. Mary [11], built in 1880, occupies the site of a twelfth century chapel. The graveyard, full of interesting stones and inscriptions, including that of Richard Watson the local poet, fronts onto Seed Hill, that part of the market where seed and grain was traded.

In 1792, John Bing visited Middleton and chronicled his stay: "Supper consisted of 'a very large trout', as the Landlord call'd it: about which trout we had a long argument; I averring 'that it was no more a trout than he was': at this he fired,' 'pray what is it, then?' - 'why a young salmon, covered with scales, who are bred in this river; and would in time get down to the sea'. Upon this excellent fish and Scotch-collops I supp'd; and soon after felt most inclined for bed, wherein I slept, like a pig, for nine hours."

So, if, after your walk, you should feel equally inclined to enjoy an excellent meal and justified repose, you may wish to complete your pleasure with a warming Courvoisier Cognac and reflect upon the countless visitors before you who have found Teesdale a 'singularly efficacious and tranquil haven for the weary traveller'.

⊂he fox's ⊂ale

nce, long ago, midst the bleak depth of a bitter December night, a bold young fox stole a goose from the run so jealously guarded by the Forester's wife. She had been fattening the bird for her families' Christmas feast and her rage the next morning, when the loss was discovered, knew no bounds.

Each day that passed she would ask her husband to set more traps and snares throughout the forest and every night all manner of animals less wily than the fox would be caught and perish in them. One evening, the Forester's daughter, collecting kindling sticks for the cooking range, strayed within the shadowy margins of the dark woods and there trod upon the open jaws of a hidden trap. Snapped shut and held by a powerful spring the crude iron teeth bit deep into her leg until her cries were heard and she was released.

The Forester, who, as steward to the Lord of the Manor, held dominion over the forests and all the beasts and foul therein, refused to set any more devices. His wife, not to be gainsaid, journeyed with the Miller to Barnard Castle on the next fair day and bought a bottle of poison from a travelling apothecarist. She harangued her husband until he agreed to use the potion to bait the carcasses of rabbits and to spread them throughout the forest to catch the fox.

Over the ensuing days, the Forester's heart was broken when he saw the grim and indiscriminate toll wrought by the poison on all manner of creatures save the foxes who now hunted a new territory, deep within the forest on the very edge of the frith itself.

"It was only a goose", he pleaded with his wife one evening. "That's as may be", she replied, "but you will not rest until I see that wicked fox with my own eyes, as dead as my poor Christmas goose."

Now it so happened that, that very same day, the fox's grandfather having lived to a great age, fell ill and returned from his distant hunting grounds to the family den to rest.

18

Content and surrounded by his family, the old fox wished that peace would once more be returned to the woodlands and, before he closed his eyes to sleep, he bade his sons, once he had no further use for it, carry his body through the frosty night and to lay it at the door of the Forester's cottage. He died peacefully later that night, just as the sickle moon cast its first dim shadow on the close cropped grass of the glade beyond.

The next morning, the Forester, who had great respect for the cunning of the old fox, and who knew that even in death the beast, who had for so long ruled the forest, would have its way and protect his family, found the body of the animal lying still beside his threshold and showed it to his wife.

"I have caught your thief for you" he lied and said no more as his wife, barely glancing up from the washing tub, observed, "Took you long enough didn't it! Now go and throw the carcass on the midden and the dogs at least shall eat their share of my poor Christmas goose".

But the Forester wrapped the old fox carefully in a piece of new sacking and buried him beside the Hudeshope Beck, on a wooded bank, just opposite the lower corn mill and overlooked from where the Foresters stands today. He placed the beast gently in the frozen ground, carefully levelling and replacing the turf lest his wife should discover the grave. "You were much nobler than I", he said quietly. He paused momentarily, then shouldering his felling axe he set off to buy his wife an extra plump goose from a farmer's wife near Laithkirk.

19

the fox's trail.

(5.5 miles, 9 kilometers, moderate walking.)

Leaving the Foresters in a northerly direction, proceed up the broad stone steps [1] to Seed Hill, and you will observe the worn stump of the old market cross, remnants of the public stocks still attached to the base, where those charged with less serious offences would endure their punishment. Justice was rough and some penalties may seem harsh by today's standards. Miners found drinking in taverns, playing cards, missing church to play football or smoking tobacco in the street could be fined the equivalent of several weeks average earnings.

Turning left from the steadily rising road to join the 'King's Walk' [2], access courtesy of the Raby Estate, the trail runs up-stream beside the Hudeshope Beck, and your footsteps join an age old tradition of local lead miners walking the lead ways to remote mines on the fells, there to remain from Monday to Saturday evening in crowded communal living quarters known as 'shops'. Each shop, where men would sleep two or more to a bunk, was governed by an elected 'king' and fostered a strong sense of comradeship between the miners.

The lime kilns on your right [3] were used to prepare locally quarried limestone as a top dressing to improve pasture land. Successive centuries of cereal cropping had, before the Enclosures and the shift in the agricultural regime, left much of the town fields and common land tired and impoverished.

Following the trail past the Miners' Bridge [4], you might imagine the rigours of a lead miner's life. The cloth 'pillow bag' or 'wallet' slung over your shoulder would carry all your food and requisites for the coming week, possibly the most precious of which, would be your supply of tallow candles, made at home from scraps of animal fat, and your only illumination at the rock face. A potential life saver too as in the case of Thomas Rowell, trapped by a rock fall in Killhope Mine in 1684, who ate his candles until the rescuers reached him.

With the Beck cascading downhill to your left, it may seem unlikely that your wallet might contain wool and knitting needles, however, most miners spent their evenings in the 'shop', gathered around the 'keggin', a communal hot water boiler, knitting, carving or embroidering fine items for sale to supplement their income.

One of the joys of recreational walking is to feel the fresh air fill one's lungs, but the majority of lead miners suffered from a variety of chronic bronchial conditions and eye complaints. Life expectancy was some fifteen years less than the national average, worse even than for the dwellers of Liverpool, recognized as the country's most unhealthy city. In mitigation, most miners held an allotment, often on high ground with poor soil, to provide them with both exercise in the open air and some much needed vegetables and vitamins to supplement their standard diet.

On your right, in the hillside, you will see some deeply incised gullies [5]. These man-made 'hushes', some of which are thousands of feet long and a hundred or more feet wide, occur widely throughout the Upper Dale. An early form of opencast mining, they were created by the damming and sudden release of water in sufficient volume to wash away the top soil and loose rock covering a seam of ore. The existence of ore was predicted by the recognition of certain land forms, telltale deposits of galena in streams, an abundance of lead tolerant vegetation such as Spring Sandwort and by dousing with traditional Hazel and Blackthorn twigs.

When you reach the metalled road [6], turn left along it, leaving the site of the Lodge Syke Mine [7] behind you and head for the ruins of the Coldberry Mine [8], the last lead workings in Teesdale, finally abandoned in 1955 having, in its long working life, produced over two thousand tons of lead ore. Please respect the fact that all old mine workings are potentially dangerous and stay on the paths.

From Coldberry you head southwards, bearing to your left [9], back towards the Miners' Bridge and Low Skears Level [4]. In this mine, the horizontal 'level' or 'adit' was driven nearly a mile into the hill towards the

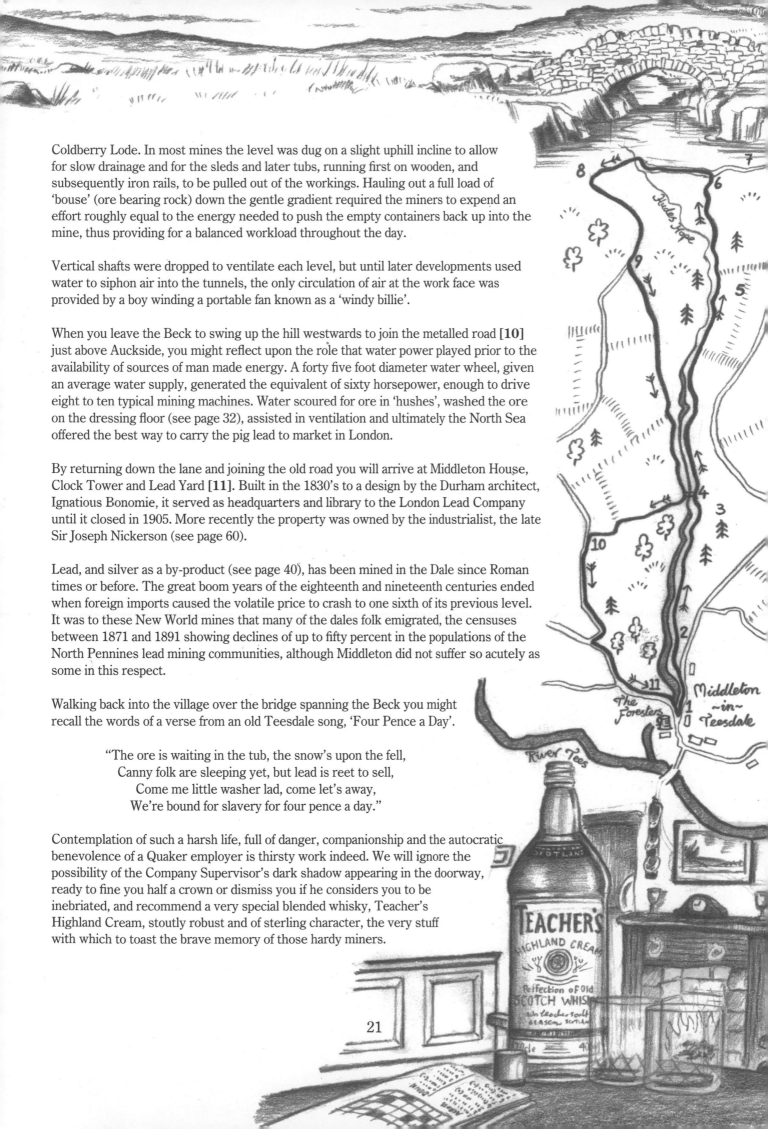

Coldberry Lode. In most mines the level was dug on a slight uphill incline to allow for slow drainage and for the sleds and later tubs, running first on wooden, and subsequently iron rails, to be pulled out of the workings. Hauling out a full load of 'bouse' (ore bearing rock) down the gentle gradient required the miners to expend an effort roughly equal to the energy needed to push the empty containers back up into the mine, thus providing for a balanced workload throughout the day.

Vertical shafts were dropped to ventilate each level, but until later developments used water to siphon air into the tunnels, the only circulation of air at the work face was provided by a boy winding a portable fan known as a 'windy billie'.

When you leave the Beck to swing up the hill westwards to join the metalled road [10] just above Auckside, you might reflect upon the role that water power played prior to the availability of sources of man made energy. A forty five foot diameter water wheel, given an average water supply, generated the equivalent of sixty horsepower, enough to drive eight to ten typical mining machines. Water scoured for ore in 'hushes', washed the ore on the dressing floor (see page 32), assisted in ventilation and ultimately the North Sea offered the best way to carry the pig lead to market in London.

By returning down the lane and joining the old road you will arrive at Middleton House, Clock Tower and Lead Yard [11]. Built in the 1830's to a design by the Durham architect, Ignatious Bonomie, it served as headquarters and library to the London Lead Company until it closed in 1905. More recently the property was owned by the industrialist, the late Sir Joseph Nickerson (see page 60).

Lead, and silver as a by-product (see page 40), has been mined in the Dale since Roman times or before. The great boom years of the eighteenth and nineteenth centuries ended when foreign imports caused the volatile price to crash to one sixth of its previous level. It was to these New World mines that many of the dales folk emigrated, the censuses between 1871 and 1891 showing declines of up to fifty percent in the populations of the North Pennines lead mining communities, although Middleton did not suffer so acutely as some in this respect.

Walking back into the village over the bridge spanning the Beck you might recall the words of a verse from an old Teesdale song, 'Four Pence a Day'.

"The ore is waiting in the tub, the snow's upon the fell,
Canny folk are sleeping yet, but lead is reet to sell,
Come me little washer lad, come let's away,
We're bound for slavery for four pence a day."

Contemplation of such a harsh life, full of danger, companionship and the autocratic benevolence of a Quaker employer is thirsty work indeed. We will ignore the possibility of the Company Supervisor's dark shadow appearing in the doorway, ready to fine you half a crown or dismiss you if he considers you to be inebriated, and recommend a very special blended whisky, Teacher's Highland Cream, stoutly robust and of sterling character, the very stuff with which to toast the brave memory of those hardy miners.

21

ᴄhe merlin's ᴄale

rom the earliest days, when tales first began to be told and to be handed down from father to son and mother to daughter, young hawks, still fledging in their warm nests, have been warned of the dangerous unpredictability of man and his children.

One wise merlin, who had hunted the hills and vales of the dale for several seasons, all the while observing man and his doings from afar, told tales of how many men would begin by wishing, and how their wishes might grow into desire; perhaps for love or gold or for gaining power over their fellow men but how, once met, their wishes achieved, they might lose interest and, at once, begin to yearn for something else in its stead.

At first the merlin could not understand how so many men could crave, achieve and then so soon appear to despise the very object of their recent ardent desire. Gradually, the bird learnt through observation, that man no longer spent all his day about the business of finding food and shelter for himself and his family, and that the more readily he could gain that which he needed, the more inclined he appeared to be to destroy that which he had wanted previously. Furthermore he came to understand that one man who owned much might merely want that which a man with less might truly need, thereby needlessly placing his fellow human in jeopardy.

The merlin had witnessed many of mans' deeds and sometimes recalled an occasion when the young son of a visiting nobleman caught sight of him soaring and spiralling in the sky above the Holwick Hills. The merlin loved to hunt the grassy sward which bordered the Green Trod, the ancient drove road leading westwards; and he remembered how the boy had cried out to his Father and to his Father's huntsman, not once but again and again with the compelling insistence of impetuous youth, "I want a hawk of my own, one to fly and hunt for me alone!"

Straight way a nest, lodged within the rugged crags of Falcon Clints, was robbed, one of the stolen eggs hatched and the hawk trained to do his young master's bidding. Though the bird pleased the youth and won fulsome praise from many an admiring hunter, the boy soon tired of the sport and desired to follow his friends and elder brothers to the lists at Richmond Castle, there to learn the noble art of jousting with the Master-at-Arms.

Early one glittering, frosty morning, a fierce North East wind blowing chill, the young nobleman, riding close by the riverbank, near where the ancient village of Unthank once stood, loosed the falcon's leather hood, slipped the thin jesses which tied him to his master's gauntlet, and tossed the blinking bird high into the bright, fast flowing air.

It soared away down wind, but seeing no quarry upon which to stoop, unable to fly against the teeth of the gale, the falcon was swept away across the bleak and frozen fells.

Without so much as a backwards glance, his youthful master turned the horse's head into the wind and rode hard for the warmth of the fire which blazed in the hall of his Uncle's hunting lodge on the bounds of Marwood Chase.

The young falcon knew not how to fend for itself and swiftly fell victim to the cold. Early one evening, not long after, the nobleman, suspecting that his son had done ill, called him to his side and, leaning forward, placed a mailed fist over one of the tallow candles, which stood before him snuffing its flame instantly and with an indifferent ease.

"How simple it is to put out a light or a life, how much more difficult to reillumin' the same." he said softly to his son.

"But Father, I only wanted... "

His Father rose abruptly, turned and strode away from where his son stood alone with his shame, whilst far above, the merlin wheeled away softly, merging silently with the gathering dusk.

23

ᚳHE ᛗERLIᚾ'S ᚠLIᚷHᚦ.

(14 miles, 22 kilometers, serious walking, with easier options. Do not attempt to cross the river between points 11 and 12 unless it is absolutely safe to do so. You return via this ford so do not cross it if the river is rising.)

This is a trail with several variations in terms of detours or overall length and you are advised, if you opt for the longer versions, to be prepared with stout footwear and waterproof clothing, the weather over the hills being prone to alter with startling suddenness.

First, however, you will have to steel yourself to quit the traditional tranquillity of the Strathmore Arms, a tavern steeped in local history and where, in the 1890's, T. H. Baharie S.A.C. a local painter, executed numerous paintings of local flora and fauna on the wooden panelled walls.

A brief northerly traverse brings you to Scorberry Bridge [1], turn up stream, remaining on the right bank, and you will come upon the Wynch Bridge [3] (see page 56). A detour to the Bowlees Visitor Centre [2] and Gibson's Cave (avid fans of the author John Buchan, please count the steps beside the quarry) is possible by crossing Scorberry Bridge and regaining the trail further upstream at the Wynch Bridge.

Soon, the gentle cascades of Low Force [4] are found. This trail is punctuated by scenic features caused by the outcropping of the hard Whin-Sill, creating High [6] and Low Force [4], Holwick [17] and Cronkley Scars [10], Falcon Clints and the cataract at Caldron Snout [12]. The molten rock was forced through faults in the limestone, which it heated, producing concentrations of minerals and areas of 'sugar limestone', the latter crucial for the survival of many rare plant species in Upper Teesdale.

High Force, best seen after rain has swollen the river, is none the less, impressive even at low flows. It tumbles seventy feet into a dark, cliff lined pool below and presents an impassable barrier to migratory fish, once so plentiful that they were raked out of the river onto the fields to rot down as a crude but effective form of pasture fertilization, and the owners of large houses often had to contract with domestic staff not to feed them with salmon more than three times each week.

Above the falls, on the left bank, lies the vast cavity of Hargreaves Quarry [7] (see page 12). The quarry is important to the local economy, shipping Whin-Sill from here to fulfill many purposes including the building of sea defences along the East Coast using giant boulders, each weighing many tons.

As you gain the pastures sheltered by Cronkley Scar [10], you have the option to turn southwards [8] joining the homeward leg of the trail at [15] on the Green Trod, the ancient drove road, beaten flat by the passage of countless thousands of cloven hooves, which linked Teesdale and the Eden Valley, or to continue westwards and then southwards, skirting the cliffs to a further option at [11] where you must decide whether to return to Holwick or to make one last detour to Caldron Snout [12] and Cow Green Reservoir [13].

This decision may be deferred a moment whilst your thoughts wander to Lake Victoria in Central Africa. An implausible thought, but Teesdale is a place where surprises and unusual connections are to be expected. To explain; just after Cronkley Bridge you passed a ruined building [9], once a slate pencil mill. Sir Roderick Murchison, president of the Royal Geographical Society in 1865, as a younger man lived in King Street, Barnard Castle and his wife a talented artist, drew geological specimens for Henry Witham of Lartington Hall.

At Rokeby Park, one evening, Sir Humphry Davy, recently contracted by the Sunderland based Society for the Prevention of Accidents in Coalmines to design a safety lamp, was much taken with Mrs. Murchison's etchings and inquired of Roderick as to his accomplishments. Roderick replied simply that he was partial to sport. Unimpressed, Sir Humphry suggested he apply himself to geology which he proceeded to do with outstanding success, achieving eminence, and organizing the expedition to the Nile which discovered the inland sea of Lake Victoria. And the pencil mill? - Sir Roderick became an expert on an ancient geological series which he called the Silurian (see page 54), named after a Celtic tribe from South-West Wales, who were contemporaries of the Brigantes. It is this same rare blue-grey stone which was quarried for slate pencils in this remote spot.

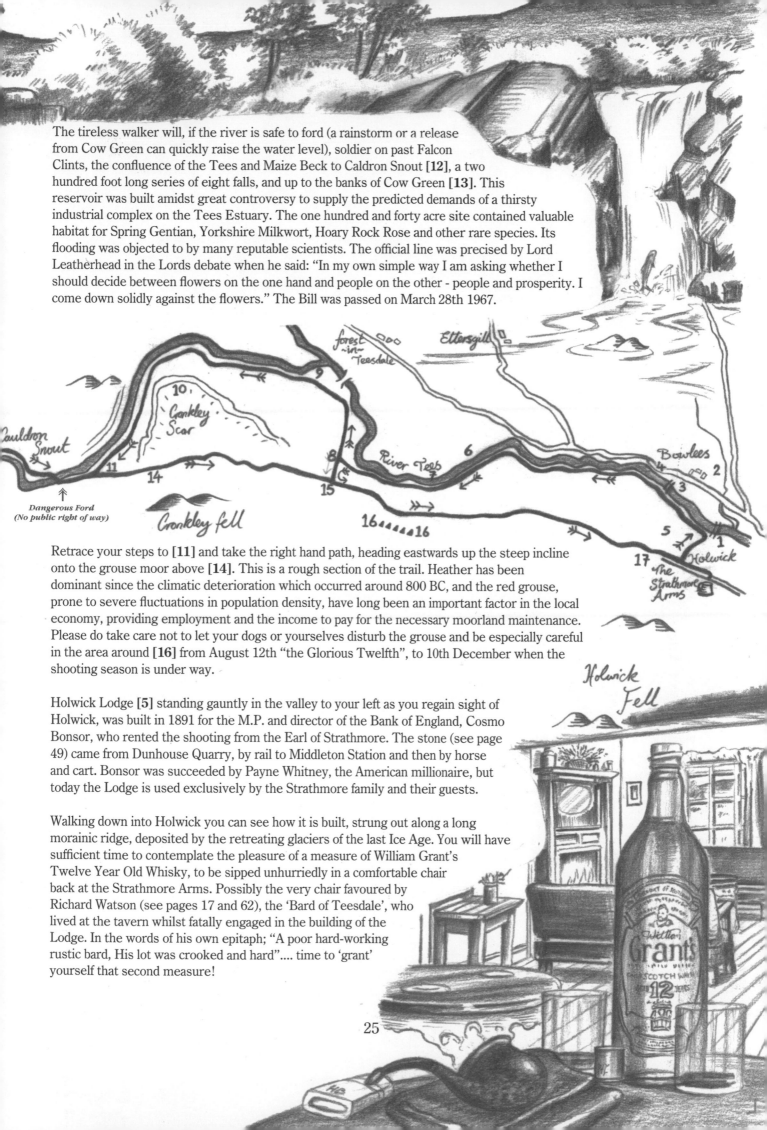

The tireless walker will, if the river is safe to ford (a rainstorm or a release from Cow Green can quickly raise the water level), soldier on past Falcon Clints, the confluence of the Tees and Maize Beck to Caldron Snout [12], a two hundred foot long series of eight falls, and up to the banks of Cow Green [13]. This reservoir was built amidst great controversy to supply the predicted demands of a thirsty industrial complex on the Tees Estuary. The one hundred and forty acre site contained valuable habitat for Spring Gentian, Yorkshire Milkwort, Hoary Rock Rose and other rare species. Its flooding was objected to by many reputable scientists. The official line was precised by Lord Leatherhead in the Lords debate when he said: "In my own simple way I am asking whether I should decide between flowers on the one hand and people on the other - people and prosperity. I come down solidly against the flowers." The Bill was passed on March 28th 1967.

Retrace your steps to [11] and take the right hand path, heading eastwards up the steep incline onto the grouse moor above [14]. This is a rough section of the trail. Heather has been dominant since the climatic deterioration which occurred around 800 BC, and the red grouse, prone to severe fluctuations in population density, have long been an important factor in the local economy, providing employment and the income to pay for the necessary moorland maintenance. Please do take care not to let your dogs or yourselves disturb the grouse and be especially careful in the area around [16] from August 12th "the Glorious Twelfth", to 10th December when the shooting season is under way.

Holwick Lodge [5] standing gauntly in the valley to your left as you regain sight of Holwick, was built in 1891 for the M.P. and director of the Bank of England, Cosmo Bonsor, who rented the shooting from the Earl of Strathmore. The stone (see page 49) came from Dunhouse Quarry, by rail to Middleton Station and then by horse and cart. Bonsor was succeeded by Payne Whitney, the American millionaire, but today the Lodge is used exclusively by the Strathmore family and their guests.

Walking down into Holwick you can see how it is built, strung out along a long morainic ridge, deposited by the retreating glaciers of the last Ice Age. You will have sufficient time to contemplate the pleasure of a measure of William Grant's Twelve Year Old Whisky, to be sipped unhurriedly in a comfortable chair back at the Strathmore Arms. Possibly the very chair favoured by Richard Watson (see pages 17 and 62), the 'Bard of Teesdale', who lived at the tavern whilst fatally engaged in the building of the Lodge. In the words of his own epitaph; "A poor hard-working rustic bard, His lot was crooked and hard".... time to 'grant' yourself that second measure!

25

the frog's tale

 ard by the Old Well Inn in Barnard Castle, stands the castle wall and below, deep in the vaulted tavern cellars, hewn from the solid bedrock itself, you will still find a vast well, part of an intricate system which fed the castle garrison with crystal clear refreshing water in time of siege.

Once, whilst a powerful and hostile army surrounded the castle, calling for its surrender, a young knight came and stood by the well alone and peaceful for a moments respite from the fierce conflict which raged above him. He cast small silver coins into the black depths, wishing aloud that his fair bride, with whom he had been wed not two months gone Michaelmas Day might know that he was thus far spared in battle and that his love for her burned undiminished. All the while, she, the daughter of a noble Yorkshire house, remained disguised and in hiding from the enemy forces within a safe sanctuary near Cotherstone, some miles without the castle walls.

So earnestly did the young knight protest his love and so saltily did his tears of anguish mingle with the pure waters of the well, that a frog took pity on his plight, and, when the grieving youth left the well side to resume his watch upon the battlements, he hopped and swam up one of the long underground culverts which fed the well from springs rising in the lush hill meadows far behind the enemy lines.

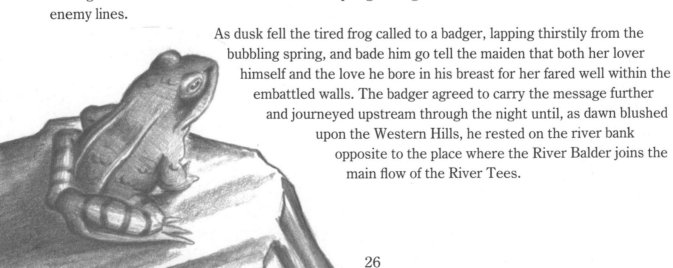

As dusk fell the tired frog called to a badger, lapping thirstily from the bubbling spring, and bade him go tell the maiden that both her lover himself and the love he bore in his breast for her fared well within the embattled walls. The badger agreed to carry the message further and journeyed upstream through the night until, as dawn blushed upon the Western Hills, he rested on the river bank opposite to the place where the River Balder joins the main flow of the River Tees.

The river was swollen by rain
which had fallen on the high
moors that night and the badger
could not swim across the flood. He called
to a dove dozing on the gnarled branch of
the old oak tree beneath which he lay.

The badger recounted the tale which the frog had
related to him and the dove, struck by the earnest of the
young knight's true wish, flew straightway to the manor
house where the maiden rested and waited, even to the
very windowsill of her chamber.

The girl was enchanted by the dove and it remained close
by, to her daily delight and comfort until, the siege being
lifted, the maiden and her steadfast lover were reunited.

Though, as husband and wife, they shared fully a score and ten
happy and fruitful years together, the knight rising in rank to
become the steward of all the local lands, he never spoke to
his lady of the time when he had visited the well in deep
despair, nor did she ever recount to him how a dove had
sustained her through her weeks of anxious solitude;
but, in their hearts, they both knew that magic had
been done in those dark days and were glad of it.

ᴄhe FROG'S QUEST.

(7 miles, 11 kilometers, easy walking, optional longer route.)

Building stone is a valuable commodity and Bernard Baliol, improving on his father Guy's original wooden fortifications on the crag at the Scar Top [1], seems, according to traditional rhyme, to have cast more than a cursory glance at the village of Marwood, where today stands the Glaxo complex and the Police Station; "Marwood was a town when Barney was nane, And Barney Castle was built wi' Marwood stane". Cat Castle Quarry in Deepdale [8] across the river probably provided the majority of the later building materials.

Leaving the Old Well, turn left up the Bank towards the octagonal Market Cross. Built in 1747 by Thomas Breaks, an accommodating structure, sometime Town Hall, jail, fire station and dairy market, its weather vane became the target of a bet in 1804 between a gamekeeper, Cruddes and a Barnard Castle Volunteer, Taylor. Both men, sporting muskets, scored hits from one hundred yards. That they escaped punishment is perhaps due to the tradition of encouraging accuracy with weapons. Henry VIII, for instance, decreed that no one over the age of twenty four should shoot a long bow at any mark from less than two hundred and twenty paces.

The clear view of St. Mary's Church was not always available until the demolition of 'Amen Corner', a block of buildings which contained Thomas Humphry's jewellers, the inspiration for Charles Dickens's 'Master Humphry's Clock'. The church, founded by Bernard Baliol in 1113, contains much of interest, including the cenotaph of one Captain Augustus Frederick Cavendish Webb of Barnard Castle and the Seventeenth Lancers, who chose "not to reason why", perishing in the Charge of the Light Brigade in the Crimea on October 25th 1854. The Bowes Museum (see page 36) is situated down Newgate.

Progress westwards through the Market Place and bear left onto the Scar Top, the old castle parade ground, when the breadth of Galgate opens to your right. Previously known more ominously as Gallows Gate or Hangslave, following the line of the Roman Road, it led to the place of public execution at its northern end [2].

The modern entrance to the Castle, enclosing over six acres within its walls, is on your left hand, but your trail slopes down into the wooded river valley and up the twenty nine stone steps [3], heading north-eastwards through Marwood Chase (see page 60), and all the way upstream, past the site of the old sulphur spring spa [4] the river and woods on your left to Cotherstone [5]. Here the Balder meets the main river, the foot bridge, originally destroyed in the flood of 1881, spanning the Tees some couple of hundred yards upstream from this confluence.

The Vikings left much evidence of their colonization south of the Tees: 'thwaite', 'force', 'gill' and suchlike appearing frequently in place names. Balder the Beautiful was, according to Norse legend, the Viking God of Innocence, son of Odin (Woden), the God of War, and Frigg. He was slain with a branch of Mistletoe by Loki, a fire demon, whilst his parents presided over Valhalla, 'the Hall of the Gods', where fallen warriors, chosen by the Valkyries, would live forever. At the Battle of Vigrid, Odin was swallowed the Fenrir Wolf, whose mighty jaws yawned agaped, touching both sky and land. According to the Fagrskinna Saga, when in 954, Eric Bloodaxe fell on Stainmore to the treachery of Earl Maccus and Oswulf of Bamburgh, Odin had himself sent two legendary warriors, Sigmund and Sinfjoli, to the gates of Valhalla to greet Eric as a bulwark against the Wolf.

At the foot bridge you must decide whether to continue along the left bank past Percymire cliff, (see page 56), up to Eggleston Bridge (Please note that this is not the site of Egglestone Abbey - see page 36), round via Romaldkirk, the Fairy Cupboards and Woden Croft (see page 58), returning to the confluence of the Tees and Balder, or to cross here and then cross the Balder below Hall Garth Hill, the site of one of the Fitz-hughs' fortified manors or castles. This one stood above the Hagg, "a remarkable natural amphitheater", the other at Ravensworth. The fortification at Cotherstone proved to be no match for the Scots raiders.

The trail leads South East, past the 1902 tomb of the tea and coffee merchant, Abraham Hilton [6], a noted local philanthropist whose will requested that his ponies should be treated as pensioners, past the mill and the Cooper House, thence to Towler Hill and past the stumps of the railway viaduct, built in 1856, to a height of one hundred and thirty two feet above the river, demolished in 1972, and on across the mouth of Deepdale and to the stone-arched County Bridge [7].

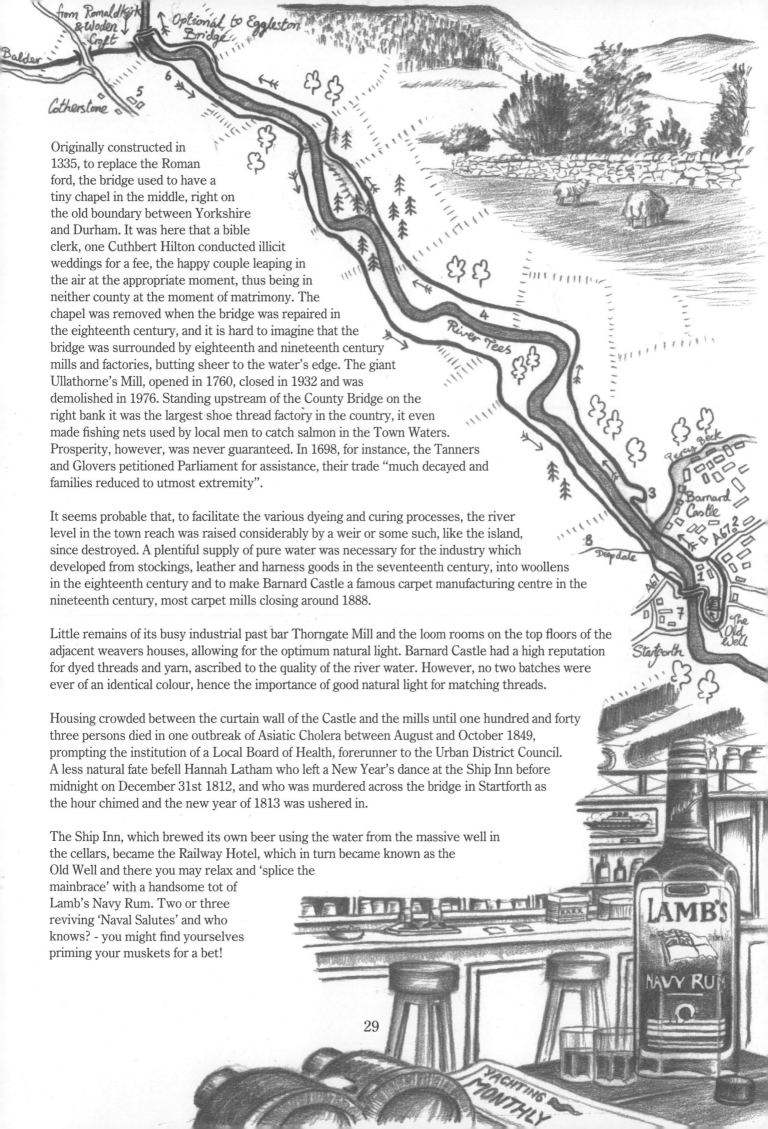

Originally constructed in 1335, to replace the Roman ford, the bridge used to have a tiny chapel in the middle, right on the old boundary between Yorkshire and Durham. It was here that a bible clerk, one Cuthbert Hilton conducted illicit weddings for a fee, the happy couple leaping in the air at the appropriate moment, thus being in neither county at the moment of matrimony. The chapel was removed when the bridge was repaired in the eighteenth century, and it is hard to imagine that the bridge was surrounded by eighteenth and nineteenth century mills and factories, butting sheer to the water's edge. The giant Ullathorne's Mill, opened in 1760, closed in 1932 and was demolished in 1976. Standing upstream of the County Bridge on the right bank it was the largest shoe thread factory in the country, it even made fishing nets used by local men to catch salmon in the Town Waters. Prosperity, however, was never guaranteed. In 1698, for instance, the Tanners and Glovers petitioned Parliament for assistance, their trade "much decayed and families reduced to utmost extremity".

It seems probable that, to facilitate the various dyeing and curing processes, the river level in the town reach was raised considerably by a weir or some such, like the island, since destroyed. A plentiful supply of pure water was necessary for the industry which developed from stockings, leather and harness goods in the seventeenth century, into woollens in the eighteenth century and to make Barnard Castle a famous carpet manufacturing centre in the nineteenth century, most carpet mills closing around 1888.

Little remains of its busy industrial past bar Thorngate Mill and the loom rooms on the top floors of the adjacent weavers houses, allowing for the optimum natural light. Barnard Castle had a high reputation for dyed threads and yarn, ascribed to the quality of the river water. However, no two batches were ever of an identical colour, hence the importance of good natural light for matching threads.

Housing crowded between the curtain wall of the Castle and the mills until one hundred and forty three persons died in one outbreak of Asiatic Cholera between August and October 1849, prompting the institution of a Local Board of Health, forerunner to the Urban District Council. A less natural fate befell Hannah Latham who left a New Year's dance at the Ship Inn before midnight on December 31st 1812, and who was murdered across the bridge in Startforth as the hour chimed and the new year of 1813 was ushered in.

The Ship Inn, which brewed its own beer using the water from the massive well in the cellars, became the Railway Hotel, which in turn became known as the Old Well and there you may relax and 'splice the mainbrace' with a handsome tot of Lamb's Navy Rum. Two or three reviving 'Naval Salutes' and who knows? - you might find yourselves priming your muskets for a bet!

29

the cat's tale

he flagstone floor, scrubbed at first light by the innkeeper's wife, glistened its warning; there being, in truth, neither man nor beast in all Butterknowle dared set foot upon her slabs whilst wet or even mildly damp. Tales tell that fierce lead smelters, carrying home a mighty thirst from the Gaunless Lead Mill, were known to stand meekly in the Stags Head forecourt ere the mistress of the house bade them enter and make merry within.

The tavern cat, curled loosely in a web of columbine, her scarcely open eyes matching the violet of the flowers on which she lounged, heard the familiar sounds of the wagonerer backing his cart to rest close by the open door.

By the low angle of the sun the cat knew the ale cart, not normally seen before the midday victuals were spread upon the polished board, to be early. From the cackling cacophony emanating from the chicken coup she knew also that the innkeeper was poaching a few choice feathers from his wife's much prized broody hen in preparation for a fishing foray that very day.

The two men conferred. The one gesturing across the still forbidden floor towards the empty oaken gantry upon which he had promised his wife to place a cask of ale before departing for his sport. The wagoner, a bachelor, pointed to the brightening sky, urging action and the other, more familiar with the imminence of domestic strife, proposed caution.

Above the gantry, itself standing so tantalizingly near the door, the wagoner contemplated a rough hewn beam of mighty girth, stoutly set about with strong iron hooks, which spanned the vaulted room.

Anxious that they should be on their way, he persuaded the innkeeper to coax the cat from her indolent repose and together they slipped a loop of silken thread, found wound on a bobbin in the wicker fishing basket, around her sleek and purring body.

The cat, famously partial to a tit-bit of cheese, sniffed the air whilst the two men cut a ripe and pungent square from their day's provisions, tied it in some muslin and hung it from the tip of a long willowy fishing pole.

Both men, giggling like children engrossed in happy mischief, manipulated the pole with its appetizing bait and thereby, drawing line all the while from the bobbin, teased the cat across the damp floor. It sprang lightly onto the ledge of the well polished dresser and up, by way of the lusterous oaken shelves, rocking but not tipping two burnished pewter platters, to the very top. From there one lissom leap and the cat, still intent on the elusive cheese, was atop the beam.

Back and forth along the beam stalked the cat following the dangling morsel until, at last, the yarn was drawn over the hook above the empty gantry. Carefully, so as not to snag and risk breaking the line, still laughing and congratulating themselves, nearly dropping the rod on one occasion, the cat, whose temper had not been improved upon its first acquaintance with a dancing cheese, was brought back safe from beam to doorway, where, in jubilation, stood the men.

In his haste, the wagoner, forgetting about the cat, pouched the parcel of muslin wrapped cheese within his leather jerkin, and set to pulling the thread to whose end the innkeeper had already attached a length of twine. Yarn pulled twine, then twine pulled rope, which, once safely drawn over the hanging hook, they lashed around the wooden keg of ale, still standing on the bed of the cart, itself now backed hard against the stone door jamb.

With a heave on the rope, the barrel swung through the air, missing the gantry by inches. Pulling swiftly the two men raised the weighty keg high above the floor, close to the beam and the violent pendulum motion changed to a languorous rotation.

Before lowering the barrel onto the gantry, the innkeeper, leaving the wagoner a moment to take the strain on the rope, sought a stout stave of sufficient length to guide the keg onto its cradle, and thereby avoid any possible disaster.

He heard a yelp of surprise and, turning swiftly, beheld the wagoner, leaping from the cart with the cat pinned to his chest. The rope disappeared unchecked into the tavern with all the ferocious energy of a striking serpent. The barrel descended, hit the gantry and bounced upwards its staves stove in, hoops loosened, bung dislodged and ale flying and spurting in unfettered abundance.

The cat, whose clawing lunge to wrest her cheese from within the wagoner's jerkin, had been the cause of the disaster, fled, not from present danger, were that not enough, but from the retribution that would surely soon descend upon them all.

"Fishing?" suggested the wagoner taking the reins. "Fishing!" agreed the innkeeper already sat beside him, and the horses, usually lazy, willingly took the strain.

That forenoon, the village carpenter, whilst repairing the gantry, paused to remark that Noah himself might have approved of this particular flood, but one glance at the innkeeper's wife, the scything arc of her busy mop and her grim stare, sufficed to council him to silence.

ThE CAt's PROWL.

(4.75 miles, 7.5 kilometers, easy walking.)

The old Stag's Head was abandoned and the present day building erected in 1909, at roughly the same time as the coal tramways were closed. The closure was prompted by the cessation of mining at the Butterknowle and Marsfield Colliery and it signalled the end of a short era of unparalleled prosperity for the area. The Haggerleases and Butterknowle branch line station, built in 1830, did not close finally until 1963.

You will observe a tramway track bed across the River Gaunless, a tributary of the River Wear, as you leave the tavern heading westwards, up the road to turn left [1] down a track, past Lower West Garth Farm, crossing the Gaunless and climbing up to the line of the old Barnard Castle railway.

The countryside all about you betrays the industrious hand of man. Unsurprisingly every square inch has been dug for coal to satisfy both domestic and industrial consumption. The Butterknowle Fault, which raises the coal-seams to the surface, stands upon the imprecise boundary between the lead mining dales and Durham Coal-field. Since the seventeenth century, coal had become increasingly vital for lead smelting (see page 40).

Following the trail through the Gibsneese Plantation, the stone chimney of the Gaunless Lead Smelting Mill [2], erected in 1832, will dominate the near horizon. This mill, built later than the Blacton Mills at Egglestone, which are known to have smelted ore as early as 1614, ceased production first, being demolished, save the chimney and manager's house [3] in the late 1890's. Packhorses bringing ore to the Gaunless Mills would carry return loads of Copley coal to Blacton to supplement the production of the Whitehouse drift colliery at Eggleston.

The chimneys were practical features introduced by Bishop Watson in 1778, in response to the widespread poisoning of the ground and waterways around the mills by lead impregnated toxic fumes and dust. He demonstrated that a flue tunnel, some running to over a mile in length, connecting furnace to chimney would allow the solids to condense, purifying substantially the emissions and recovering quantities of lead when the flues were flushed with water. The Gaunless chimney was built close to the mill and the flue followed a zig-zag pattern to increase its length. Later technological advances allowed for the construction of condensation chambers and the use of water to cool the fumes. The last chimney at the Blacton Mill, a fine octagonal structure, was demolished in 1932.

Passing through this pleasant wooded valley, it is not easy to imagine the privations suffered by those employed in the lead mining industry (see page 20), and particularly so in the early days. The toxicity was not limited to the environs of the smelting sites. Lead dust covered the miners cloths and permeated every stage of the dressing process, where women and children would create 'Smithson', by separating and washing the ore from the 'bouse'. The dust from concentrated ore would then poison the lead ways as it was transported to the smelt mills. All such contaminated land was known as 'bellund ground'.

Imagine as you leave the stream and head northwards, crossing the metalled road past Lane Head [4], to where you swing eastwards on the home leg, that you are a 'jagger', the owner of a string of twelve to twenty pack ponies, strong, stocky Galloways or 'Gals'. The beasts stood a little under fourteen hands high and carried iron framed, wooden saddles. Each pony was muzzled to prevent it snatching a fatal mouthful of contaminated grass along the trail and the unmuzzled lead horse carried a bell on its harness. These packhorse strings, along with all the plough and wagon horses from the farms kept many a blacksmith busy (see page 40).

Cargo, whether coal, pig lead, smithson, or whatever you had been contracted to haul, was carried in leather saddle bags, two per animal, each bag capable of carrying one 'bing' or hundredweight, so that ten ponies would transport approximately one ton. Poor weather could render most of the tracks impassable and it was this unpredictability and inefficiency which encouraged advances in the road and rail systems (see page 13).

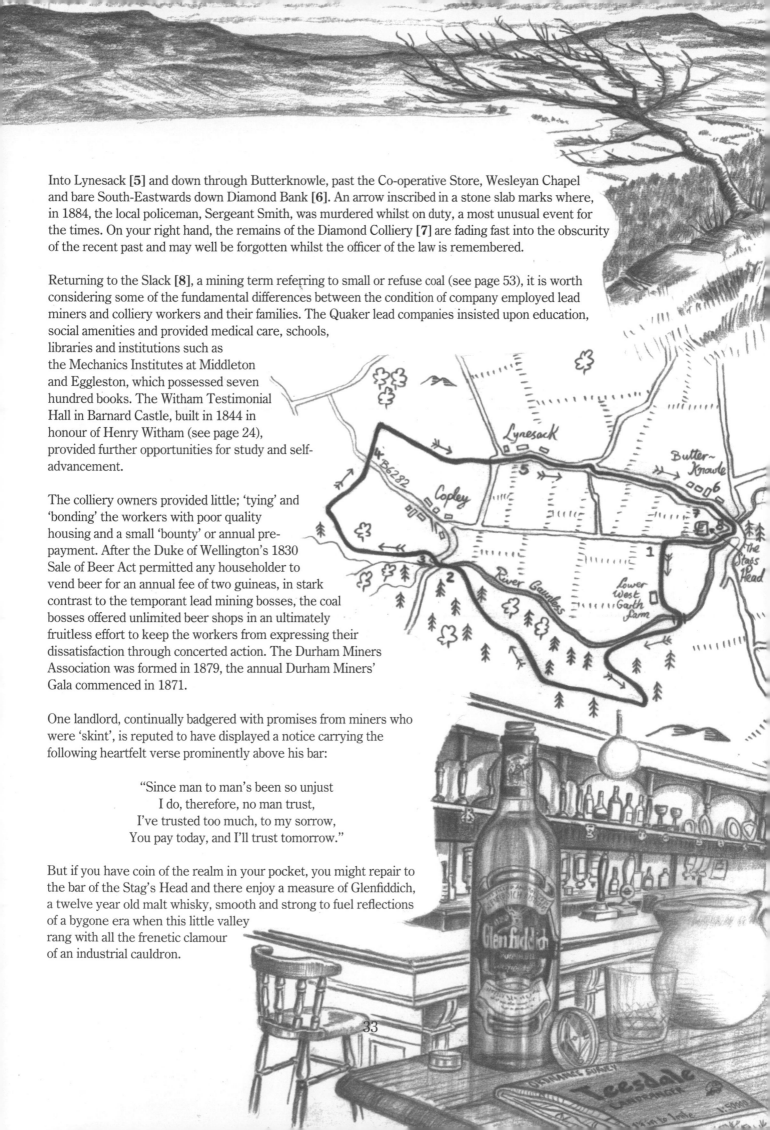

Into Lynesack [5] and down through Butterknowle, past the Co-operative Store, Wesleyan Chapel and bare South-Eastwards down Diamond Bank [6]. An arrow inscribed in a stone slab marks where, in 1884, the local policeman, Sergeant Smith, was murdered whilst on duty, a most unusual event for the times. On your right hand, the remains of the Diamond Colliery [7] are fading fast into the obscurity of the recent past and may well be forgotten whilst the officer of the law is remembered.

Returning to the Slack [8], a mining term referring to small or refuse coal (see page 53), it is worth considering some of the fundamental differences between the condition of company employed lead miners and colliery workers and their families. The Quaker lead companies insisted upon education, social amenities and provided medical care, schools, libraries and institutions such as the Mechanics Institutes at Middleton and Eggleston, which possessed seven hundred books. The Witham Testimonial Hall in Barnard Castle, built in 1844 in honour of Henry Witham (see page 24), provided further opportunities for study and self-advancement.

The colliery owners provided little; 'tying' and 'bonding' the workers with poor quality housing and a small 'bounty' or annual pre-payment. After the Duke of Wellington's 1830 Sale of Beer Act permitted any householder to vend beer for an annual fee of two guineas, in stark contrast to the temporant lead mining bosses, the coal bosses offered unlimited beer shops in an ultimately fruitless effort to keep the workers from expressing their dissatisfaction through concerted action. The Durham Miners Association was formed in 1879, the annual Durham Miners' Gala commenced in 1871.

One landlord, continually badgered with promises from miners who were 'skint', is reputed to have displayed a notice carrying the following heartfelt verse prominently above his bar:

> "Since man to man's been so unjust
> I do, therefore, no man trust,
> I've trusted too much, to my sorrow,
> You pay today, and I'll trust tomorrow."

But if you have coin of the realm in your pocket, you might repair to the bar of the Stag's Head and there enjoy a measure of Glenfiddich, a twelve year old malt whisky, smooth and strong to fuel reflections of a bygone era when this little valley rang with all the frenetic clamour of an industrial cauldron.

33

the kingfisher's tale

One morning in early Spring, the River Tees was full of large, fresh run salmon, returning from years spent at sea feeding on the riches of the fertile ocean waters which lap the shores of far-away Greenland. The river flow was low, reduced to a mere trickle by the drought, and the deep pools alone played sanctuary to the shoals of fish, awaiting impatiently for a flood upon which to run further upstream and, thereby, to gain access to the gravel filled spawning redds.

In one such pool, close to the spot where a bridge now spans the river at Whorlton, the salmon became so restless that an elder, fearing that the oxygen starved fish might begin to fight amongst themselves, sought a diversion for them.

He rose to the surface and scanned the azure sky, He espied one small whisp of cloud, powder pink in the glow of the climbing sun, and cried out, "Little cloud, go tell your dark and lowering brothers that we need the gift of their rain to swell our river." The cloud replied, "Mighty silver salmon, what shall I tell my thunder brothers to cause them to heed your plea?"

"Tell them", replied the noble fish, "Tell them that all the fish, the foul and the beasts of the river shall each tell a story or sing a song." The salmon knew well that clouds love an open air entertainment and that they will travel miles to fill the sky as news of one is spread abroad.

The tiny cloud drifted away on a light breeze and the fish spread the word up and down the length of the river bank that a competition would be held at noon that day. As the sun rose to its zenith the salmon, trapped in the pool jostled and sulked, each vying for a shady position or a cool flow of water, whilst above all manner of creature flew, ran and swam to the contest.

By midday, as if by magic, the sky darkened and the heavy clouds, for so long absent, gathered to enjoy the spectacle. The salmon leapt to greet the clouds with a graceful curve of his powerful tail and thus signalled that the contest should begin.

Pairs of mallard sang love duets, otters told epic tales of wars and heroic deeds, grayling danced the polka with elegantly attired mayflies and, as every successive creature performed, the clouds,

34

enraptured, jostled closer and closer together, shrouding ever darkening the stage below. Each turn was greeted with rumbles of thunder and each bow applauded with a dazzling flash of lightning. At last, all had performed save the drab and colourless little kingfisher, who sat shyly and inconspicuously on a twig, overhanging the waterfall. Urged on by the salmon and the other creatures, the bird began to recall a dream, a vision of portentous warning.

The kingfisher spoke of times to come, when man would gain knowledge and thereby power over the natural world. He foretold that man would build huge walls of earth and stone across the river valleys, impounding the tributary waters, stemming floods and denying historic spawning grounds to the fish. He prophesied that man would plant great forests on the headwaters and fill each estuary with poison, that he would drain the moors and thereby choke the riverbed with silt.

The tiny bird paused for breath but the clouds could contain their sorrow no more. Before he could continue his tale, the clouds began to weep, their tears falling as raindrops, cascading down as heavily as rain has ever fallen upon the earth before. The deluge swelled the river which rose in a mighty spate, freeing the trapped salmon to run the tumbling currents once more.

Eventually, the sad clouds were exhausted and a watery sun broke through. The noble salmon called to the kingfisher, "Fly through the rainbow and you will be rewarded for your tale. Fly now and all the colours of the prism will belong to you and to your children forever and lightning will dance upon your wings!" The bird flew, and it came to pass just as the fish had promised and the kingfisher's plumage radiated every shimmering hue in the broad vaulted celestial palette.

the kingfisher's kingdom.

(5.5 miles, 9 kilometers, easy walking.)

Leave the Bridge Inn, heading southwards through the broad village green, with the Jubilee Fountain and church of St. Mary, rebuilt in 1853 on Saxon foundations. The central enclosure formed by the original buildings is typical of a 'green village', designed to accommodate livestock within a defensible perimeter, an early lesson for wagon masters passing through Indian Territory in America's mid-west. Most Durham 'green villages' are orientated on an east - west axis and are more linear in shape than Whorlton.

Just above the river Tees, as the road drops away to the your left, you bear right [1] and follow the left bank of the river upstream, using the tranquility of the setting to prepare yourselves for the cultural feast of truly heroic proportions which lies ahead; and which begins as you pass the old corn mill [2] on the Demesnes (the Manorial Farm) still in use as late as the 1930's. Here the Lord of the Manor enjoyed a monopoly on the grinding of corn and levied his tax of one sixteenth by weight, the miller also deducting his fee or 'multure'. The Demesnes were the lands owned by the Manor and worked by the people, their labour counting as a further form of taxation paid to the Lord (see page 16).

Further upstream, John Bayles, another miller, whose mill stood by the river close to Romaldkirk (see pages 28 and 40), is thought to have carried a plague into that village and the surrounding area from Newcastle in 1636. The village was devastated, the Rector, Curate and Clerk succumbing. The church was closed and the dead were carted away to be buried on Croft Yokes field without the last rights.

Climbing the slope and passing through a kissing gate into the lane known as Parson's Lonnen, the John and Josephine Bowes Museum [3] (see page 62) stands in all its magnificence across the road, the gates slightly to your right. Designed by Joules Pellachet and, due to French political instability caused by the Franco-Prussian war, Calais being the originally chosen site, the museum was built close to John's family home at Streatlam Castle. It was opened in 1892, sadly after the death of both John and Josephine, his French actress wife. The collections, buildings and setting demand that you visit and linger here awhile and share in this living memorial to an epic and noble romance.

Back on the trail, progress down Newgate (the word 'gate' indicated originally a street and not a gateway as might be supposed) to the Market Cross [4] (see page 28), left down the Bank, once so steep that pedestrians used a set of steps cut into the side of the road. Pause at the Old Well for refreshment if so desired, and then proceed straight on through Thorngate, the site of the Chapel of the Sacred Thorn, past the weavers houses and the mill (see page 24), across the Green Bridge [5], the previous structure being swept away in the flood of 1881 with two over enthusiastic spectators on board, and safely back on terra firma and the right bank of the river at Low Startforth.

Head downstream towards the Lendings, where once stood a cloth mill, opposite the old corn mill, and detour around to the south of the Lendings Caravan Park, arriving at the ancient pack horse bridge [6] over Thorsgill Beck and the noble, cruciform ruins of Egglestone Abbey [7], founded in 1195 by Ralph Nulton. The Premostratensian order of White Cannons were poorly endowed and enjoyed an uneasy relationship with the townsfolk, secreting daggers beneath their unusual white habits. The Monastery and Abbey were dissolved in 1540 and the building fell into disrepair, being used at one time, after the proper drying shed had been burnt down in 1816, to dry paper produced by a mill whose ruins stand behind the adjacent farmhouse. The Abbey ruins and the mill are depicted on a watercolour by Turner.

The trail passes the southern end of the Abbey Bridge [8] built in 1773 with funds from J. Morritt. Tolls were charged on a tariff, with livestock counted by the score (in twenties), and collected by the bridge keeper, whose bedroom was built on the upstream side, and whose living room was built on the downstream side, from where Paradise Walk leads to Rokeby Park [9], a private residence open to the public at specific times (see page 68).

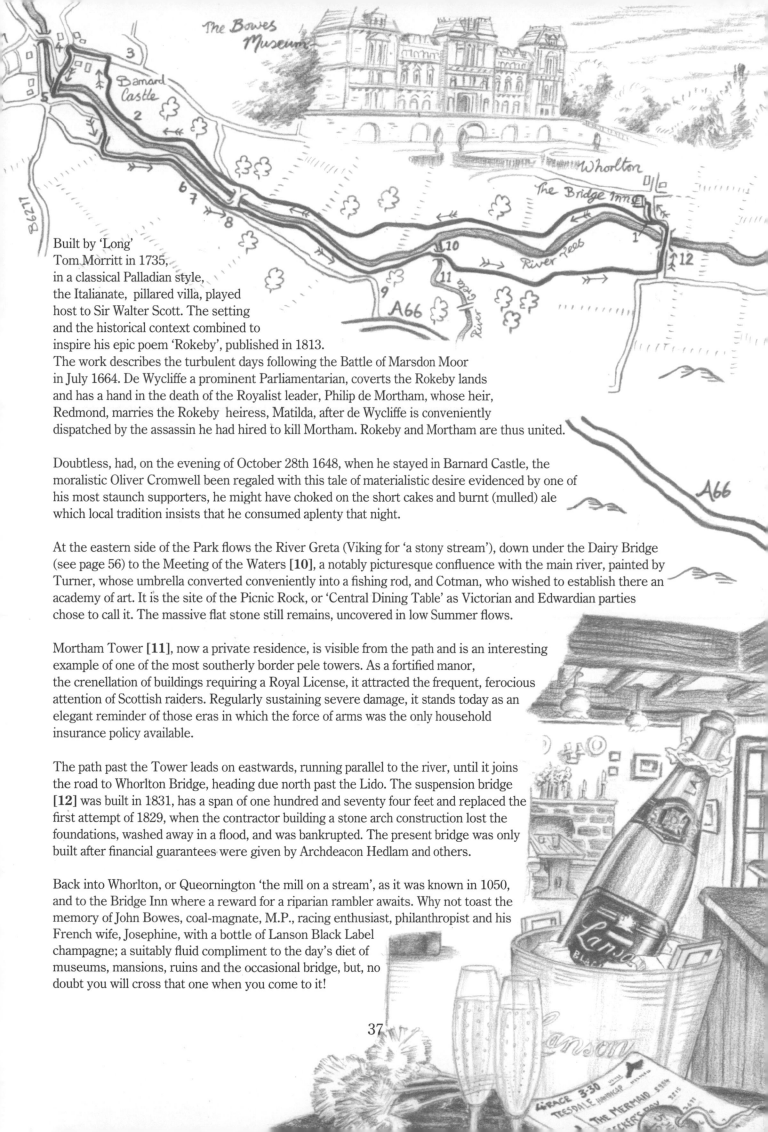

Built by 'Long' Tom Morritt in 1735, in a classical Palladian style, the Italianate, pillared villa, played host to Sir Walter Scott. The setting and the historical context combined to inspire his epic poem 'Rokeby', published in 1813. The work describes the turbulent days following the Battle of Marsdon Moor in July 1664. De Wycliffe a prominent Parliamentarian, coverts the Rokeby lands and has a hand in the death of the Royalist leader, Philip de Mortham, whose heir, Redmond, marries the Rokeby heiress, Matilda, after de Wycliffe is conveniently dispatched by the assassin he had hired to kill Mortham. Rokeby and Mortham are thus united.

Doubtless, had, on the evening of October 28th 1648, when he stayed in Barnard Castle, the moralistic Oliver Cromwell been regaled with this tale of materialistic desire evidenced by one of his most staunch supporters, he might have choked on the short cakes and burnt (mulled) ale which local tradition insists that he consumed aplenty that night.

At the eastern side of the Park flows the River Greta (Viking for 'a stony stream'), down under the Dairy Bridge (see page 56) to the Meeting of the Waters [10], a notably picturesque confluence with the main river, painted by Turner, whose umbrella converted conveniently into a fishing rod, and Cotman, who wished to establish there an academy of art. It is the site of the Picnic Rock, or 'Central Dining Table' as Victorian and Edwardian parties chose to call it. The massive flat stone still remains, uncovered in low Summer flows.

Mortham Tower [11], now a private residence, is visible from the path and is an interesting example of one of the most southerly border pele towers. As a fortified manor, the crenellation of buildings requiring a Royal License, it attracted the frequent, ferocious attention of Scottish raiders. Regularly sustaining severe damage, it stands today as an elegant reminder of those eras in which the force of arms was the only household insurance policy available.

The path past the Tower leads on eastwards, running parallel to the river, until it joins the road to Whorlton Bridge, heading due north past the Lido. The suspension bridge [12] was built in 1831, has a span of one hundred and seventy four feet and replaced the first attempt of 1829, when the contractor building a stone arch construction lost the foundations, washed away in a flood, and was bankrupted. The present bridge was only built after financial guarantees were given by Archdeacon Hedlam and others.

Back into Whorlton, or Queornington 'the mill on a stream', as it was known in 1050, and to the Bridge Inn where a reward for a riparian rambler awaits. Why not toast the memory of John Bowes, coal-magnate, M.P., racing enthusiast, philanthropist and his French wife, Josephine, with a bottle of Lanson Black Label champagne; a suitably fluid compliment to the day's diet of museums, mansions, ruins and the occasional bridge, but, no doubt you will cross that one when you come to it!

the mouse's tale

s the staccato clatter of iron shod horses hooves on the worn cobbles faded into the gathering night, the Mickleton blacksmith sat with his head in his hands, a picture of abject misery, silhouetted against the ruddy glow of the forge's furnace. On the worn anvil before him lay a piece of parchment, in the bottom corner affixed a heavy red wax seal. Haltingly the blacksmith read and reread the somber words by the flickering light of the fire.

Later, he gathered his wife and young daughters to his side, and, with the forge mice watching and listening intently from the safety of the blackened oak rafters, he spoke slowly and softly; telling them that the very next day the Sheriff and his officers, so recently departed, would return to evict them. He explained how the business had suffered badly from his illness, which still, after these many months, could leave him too weak to wield the heavy hammers or pump the bellows, and how, as a consequence, the rent of two gold pieces had not been earned and could not be paid. As the blacksmith placed his strong and honest arms around his weeping family the mice scuttled back to their nest in great alarm.

The mice knew well that the new blacksmith would almost certainly be the baker's brother, and that no mice lived at or even close by the bakery, but rather two savage cats and a litter of hungry kittens, some of whom would be sure to come and live at the forge.

The elder mouse, finishing a piece of the blacksmith's cheese with undisguised relish, wiped his long whiskers thoughtfully and with great care, flicked the tip of this pink tail and, ready at last, he spoke; "My fellow forge dwellers", he began; "We must either help our friend the kind and gentle blacksmith, or prepare to leave our home tomorrow too!"

All the assembled mice nodded in agreement and the smallest mouse timidly raised a paw

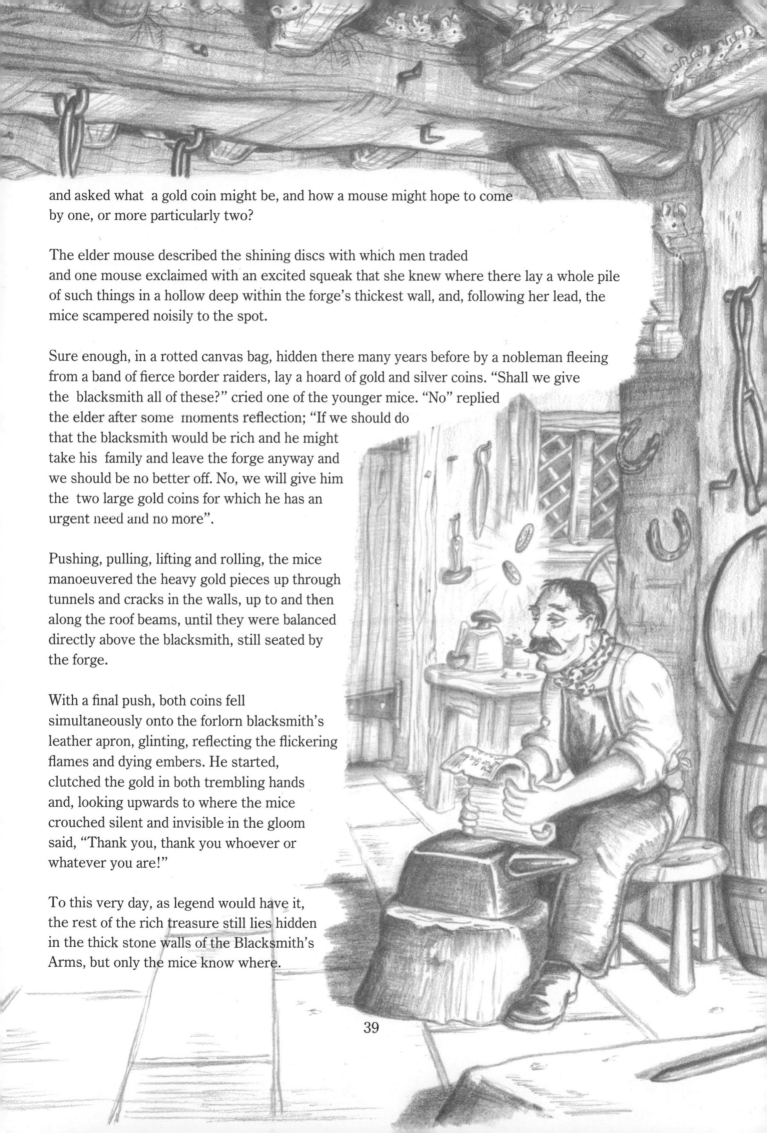

and asked what a gold coin might be, and how a mouse might hope to come by one, or more particularly two?

The elder mouse described the shining discs with which men traded and one mouse exclaimed with an excited squeak that she knew where there lay a whole pile of such things in a hollow deep within the forge's thickest wall, and, following her lead, the mice scampered noisily to the spot.

Sure enough, in a rotted canvas bag, hidden there many years before by a nobleman fleeing from a band of fierce border raiders, lay a hoard of gold and silver coins. "Shall we give the blacksmith all of these?" cried one of the younger mice. "No" replied the elder after some moments reflection; "If we should do that the blacksmith would be rich and he might take his family and leave the forge anyway and we should be no better off. No, we will give him the two large gold coins for which he has an urgent need and no more".

Pushing, pulling, lifting and rolling, the mice manoeuvered the heavy gold pieces up through tunnels and cracks in the walls, up to and then along the roof beams, until they were balanced directly above the blacksmith, still seated by the forge.

With a final push, both coins fell simultaneously onto the forlorn blacksmith's leather apron, glinting, reflecting the flickering flames and dying embers. He started, clutched the gold in both trembling hands and, looking upwards to where the mice crouched silent and invisible in the gloom said, "Thank you, thank you whoever or whatever you are!"

To this very day, as legend would have it, the rest of the rich treasure still lies hidden in the thick stone walls of the Blacksmith's Arms, but only the mice know where.

the mouse's epic.

(5 miles, 8 kilometers, easy walking.)

Blacksmiths forges or 'smithies' were the equivalent to today's garages, servicing and repairing the various methods of transportation, and particularly those aspects pertaining to horse power (see page 32). The shoeing of beasts, repairs to iron bound wagon wheel rims, wheelwrights being less common than blacksmiths, and the essential ability to maintain and repair both weapons and the basic agricultural and industrial machinery of the time implied that every settlement of any consequence would contain at least one forge.

From the door of the Blacksmiths Arms in Mickleton, a working smithy having stood here from the seventeenth century or earlier, becoming first a working man's club at the turn of the century and then an inn, the trail leads directly south. Passing a picnic site [1] where the steam railway station stood, over a bridge crossing the old track bed, past a disused quarry, one side used for land fill, the other a clay pigeon shooting facility (see page 68), the trail leads up over a series of blind summits and onto Bail Hill [2].

The name 'Bale', 'Bole' or 'Baal' usually denoted the presence of an early lead smelting hearth. The crudely constructed furnace would be sighted wherever the maximum constant draught could be expected. The air supply was vital for a successful smelt, each firing taking upwards of twelve hours to burn through the mixture of 'smithsan' (see page 32), peat and or coal or charcoal. Optimum conditions for a hearth were often found on the tops or upper windward slopes of hills, or beside fast streams where water wheels could power bellows.

Efficiency was paramount for successful mining. The 'bouse' (see page 21) contained a five to ten percent ore content. This was increased to a seventy percent concentration by the dressers before smelting. Transportation was costly and unreliable so minimum volume carried over minimum distance was the key. A smelting hearth and the dressing floor, where conditions would allow, would be grouped close to the portal of the level.

At the top of Scarney Hill [3], just past the the incongruous intrusion of the modern transmitter mast, the trail turns sharp right and eastwards across Romaldkirk Moor. If you chose the left turn you will descend into the village of Romaldkirk, with its Saxon church, dedicated to the infant St. Romald, known as 'the Cathedral of the Dales'. A past Rector, Owen Oglethorpe, President of Magdalen College, Oxford for nineteen years, became Bishop of Carlisle in 1557 and crowned Queen Elizabeth I in 1558.

The village was frequently sacked and in 1070 the Scottish King Malcolm III slaughtered a large number of dales men at the Battle of Hunderthwaite. No doubt the Scots considered silverware attractive booty, highly valuable and easy to carry. Silver had been extracted from lead mines since pre-Roman times by a process involving the secondary smelting of refined lead. The resulting total oxidization of the lead produced litharge and a residual quantity of silver cake. In 1833, Hugh Patterson, working at the Blacton Mill, Egglestone (see page 32), developed a less wasteful process using the varying properties of crystallization, his advance being rapidly superseded by the Rogan Patient of 1870.

At Botany [4], leave the moor land track and turning to the right, head northwards down the slope, bearing left after half a mile to arrive at the visitor centre near the Grassholme Reservoir dam [5]. The six main reservoirs in Teesdale offer a massive combined capacity for water storage and represent some significant civil engineering triumphs of their day. One example, like so many, completely hidden from the eye is the two mile long tunnel connecting Grassholme to the Hury Reservoir in Baldersdale. In places three hundred and fifty feet below ground, the dimensions are six feet high by three and three quarters feet wide. Probably no coincidence that these are the same measurements as are found in lead mine levels.

These impoundations of water, and consequential barriers across historic spawning tributaries are the source of much debate. Their presence modifies the natural effects of water mechanics within the catchment, lessening the scour of flash floods, creating micro-climates, and providing a wealth of leisure facilities (see page 68) for residents and visitors alike.

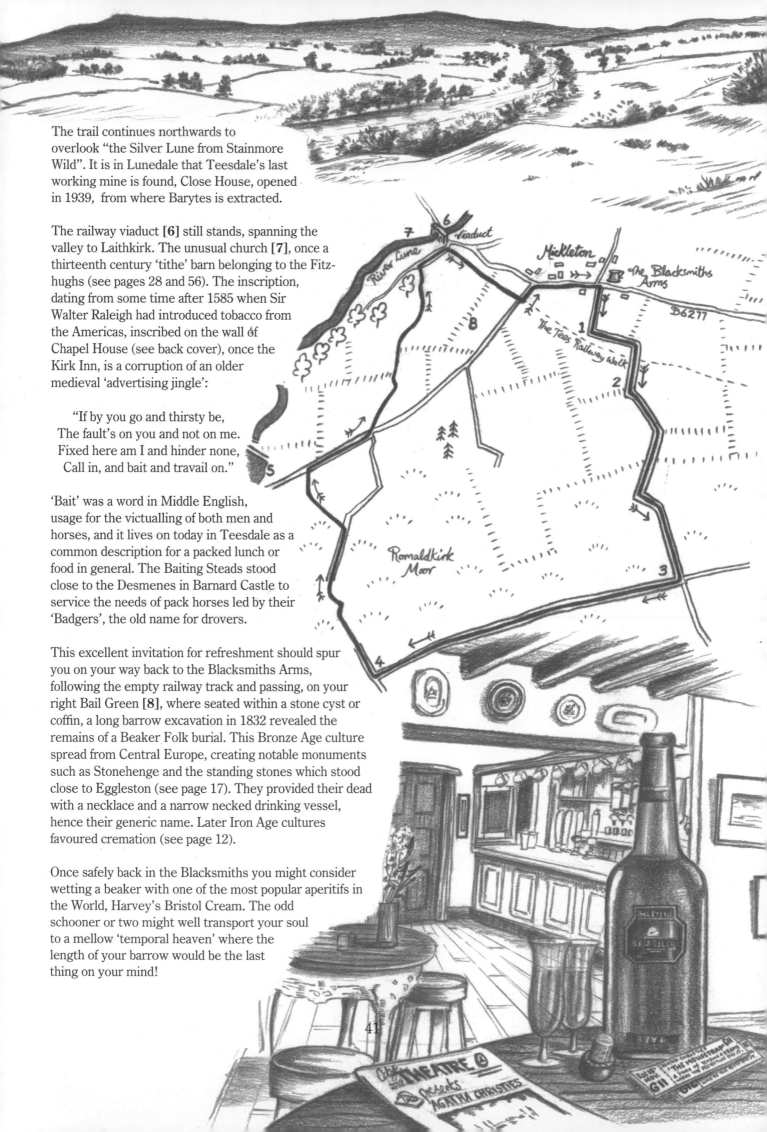

The trail continues northwards to overlook "the Silver Lune from Stainmore Wild". It is in Lunedale that Teesdale's last working mine is found, Close House, opened in 1939, from where Barytes is extracted.

The railway viaduct **[6]** still stands, spanning the valley to Laithkirk. The unusual church **[7]**, once a thirteenth century 'tithe' barn belonging to the Fitzhughs (see pages 28 and 56). The inscription, dating from some time after 1585 when Sir Walter Raleigh had introduced tobacco from the Americas, inscribed on the wall of Chapel House (see back cover), once the Kirk Inn, is a corruption of an older medieval 'advertising jingle':

> "If by you go and thirsty be,
> The fault's on you and not on me.
> Fixed here am I and hinder none,
> Call in, and bait and travail on."

'Bait' was a word in Middle English, usage for the victualling of both men and horses, and it lives on today in Teesdale as a common description for a packed lunch or food in general. The Baiting Steads stood close to the Desmenes in Barnard Castle to service the needs of pack horses led by their 'Badgers', the old name for drovers.

This excellent invitation for refreshment should spur you on your way back to the Blacksmiths Arms, following the empty railway track and passing, on your right Bail Green **[8]**, where seated within a stone cyst or coffin, a long barrow excavation in 1832 revealed the remains of a Beaker Folk burial. This Bronze Age culture spread from Central Europe, creating notable monuments such as Stonehenge and the standing stones which stood close to Eggleston (see page 17). They provided their dead with a necklace and a narrow necked drinking vessel, hence their generic name. Later Iron Age cultures favoured cremation (see page 12).

Once safely back in the Blacksmiths you might consider wetting a beaker with one of the most popular aperitifs in the World, Harvey's Bristol Cream. The odd schooner or two might well transport your soul to a mellow 'temporal heaven' where the length of your barrow would be the last thing on your mind!

CHE PARCRIDGE'S CALE

n the olden days, long before agricultural chemicals killed the insects and machines began to plough and harvest the rich lands around Caldwell, the grasslands and the stubble fields abounded with large coveys of plump gray partridge, providing sport and delicate dishes to be served at the tables of the local gentry.

The huntsmen would employ two breeds of dog to aid them capture their chosen quarry; sending out pointers or setters upwind to quarter the ground in front of them. When the pointers scented a covey they would approach and go 'on point', standing stretched out stiffly, lent slightly forward, nose to the quarry, front paw raised and tail horizontal to the ground. Once the guns had closed, on command, the pointers would move forward slowly to flush the birds into the air.

The setters on the other hand, once scenting a covey near by, would sink to the ground and, by inching forward, 'held' the quarry still whilst the crouching huntsmen would creep up behind carrying a weighted net to cast over both the partridge and the dogs on the ground.

A young bird had observed these tactics and spoke to his friends, suggesting a plan to thwart the success of the huntsmen. The covey agreed, and the very next day two pointers scented the group hidden in a cluster of tussocks. As the heads of the guns came into view and the dogs began to move again the young partridge cried; "Run, run for your lives but do not fly!". The covey separated, birds running hither and thither and the dogs and the guns were left in total confusion.

42

The same week, a party with nets and setters came across the covey and, as the setters crouched downwind, the netsmen closing, the young partridge cried; "Fly, fly for your lives," and the frightened birds rose into the air as the net spread out below them covering the dogs and their roost so timely vacated.

At first the hunters were bewildered and, as the fame of the elusive covey spread, this turned to great respect mingled with no little good humour. The health of the young bird that led the covey was toasted heartily at many a hunting banquet.

Not all men, however, in any age of history, share true empathy with their quarry; and one such, on a late December morning, followed a party of netsmen and their setters. He was armed with a flintlock and, as the covey rose above the unfolding net, he shot the leader even as it issued its shrill cry of warning, a thin reedy call, drowned by the roar of the fowling piece discharging.

The Lord of the Manor was angry and banished the hunter from his lands forever, instructing the wife of his most trusted squire to employ all her cunning and dexterity to preserve the bird in its natural form.

Just before dawn that Christmas morning, quietly, the partridge was placed upon the bough of an ornamental fruit tree which graced his Lady's chamber. When she awoke, her delight knew no bounds and she commanded a travelling troubadour to record her pleasure in a song. He sang that night, after the raucous jollity of the Yule feast had died down.

It is possible that you may have heard the song he sang, and if you have you will know now just how the brave young partridge came to grace a Lady's pear tree.

43

the partridge's progress.

(6 miles, 9.5 kilometers, easy walking.)

Leave the Brownlow Arms, settled snugly beneath the spreading chestnut boughs which once shaded the turnpike, linking the coalfields of Cockfield Fell and Butterknowle to the hungry markets of Richmond, and head southeast briefly before turning north [1] to pass Slough Hill on the way to High Close. Turn left on to Pudding Hill Road and then sharp right, northwards again, onto Boat Lane, leading towards Gainford across the River Tees from the old ruined ferry station, the fare being one old penny each way.

Had you ignored the first left hand turn, the road from the Brownlow would have led you to Forcett and beyond. A branch of the railway line spurred off some way east of Gainford and linked the quarries at Forcett to the iron smelting furnaces in Darlington and Cleveland, which used the high quality limestone as flux. Teesdale, particularly Lunedale and the Upper Dale, contains appreciable deposits of iron ore, but its extraction and smelting never matched the importance of the iron industry in neighbouring Weardale. In 1235, Ranulf was accorded half the iron from the forges and half the smelting furnaces in the Forest of Lunedale. The commercial exploitation of the deposits was last seriously evaluated during the Second World War.

To the east of Forcett lie the extensive earthworks of Stanwick-St.-John, where, in 1844 a hoard of bronze axes and spearheads, horse harnesses, iron chariot wheel rims and many other artifacts, were unearthed. The complex of banks and ditches encloses some eight hundred acres and may have been part of a larger defensive system, known as the 'Scots Dyke', running from Richmond in the south, across the River Swale to Old Richmond on the southern bank of the Tees. The purpose and even the creators of these more extensive fortifications are shrouded in considerable mystery. They offer no strategic strength, possibly marking a temporary frontier.

The Brigantes (see page 12) certainly used Stanwick-St.-John, until subdued by Agricola's Ninth Roman Legion around 80 AD. Agricola's exploits are well documented because Tacitus was his son-in-law. The Romans, established a fortress at Piercebridge to guard the bridge carrying Dere Street across the Tees, Binchester similarly guarding this York to Corbridge supply route where it crosses the River Wear. An interesting recent theory suggests that heavy supplies may have been shipped inland by shallow draft barges to such points, overcoming the logistical problems associated with long distance haulage by ox cart. Much later, the Vikings may have emulated this pattern of colonization when they established their strategic inland river side bases. A reverse barge system would later carry coal to the staiths at the river estuaries (see page 53).

Back to Boat Lane. The trail branches left [2] towards the ruins of St. Lawrence's Chapel before the lane reaches the old ferry station. Gainford, the town it served, standing on the north bank, was once the centre of administration for the Dale as far west as Middleton. The original Saxon church used stone from the Piercebridge fortress, and the town was bought by the Vanes of Raby in 1634. In Victorian and Edwardian times a sulphur spring [3] became a fashionable spa, causing an increase of visitors to the area.

St. Lawrence's Chapel [4] was built in the thirteenth century and its remains stand on the site of the vanished village of Barford or Old Richmond, the village stone being robbed by the cartload for use at other sites. The tower shaped dove cote, standing to the north of the chapel, belongs to the Manor House, another dilapidated cote standing in the grounds of the unaltered Jacobean Gainford Hall [5], completed in 1605. Pigeon and particularly tender squabs, their young, offered a welcome variation to the fare on many a Baronial table.

The sorry inhabitants of another tower, The Tower of London, might occupy your mind as the trail swings round, west and then southwest, to follow the curve of the river bed. Indeed the keen observer of Ordnance Survey maps may have wondered why the Barnard Castle to Darlington railway line should deviate from its course, crossing temporarily, south of the river, over two costly bridges. The reason being that the then Duke of Cleveland, ancestor of the present Lord Barnard, did not wish the park at Selaby Hall [6], once the home of Lord Brackenbury, King Richard III's Constable of the Tower, to be disturbed. The Hall is visible on the high ground across the river .

44

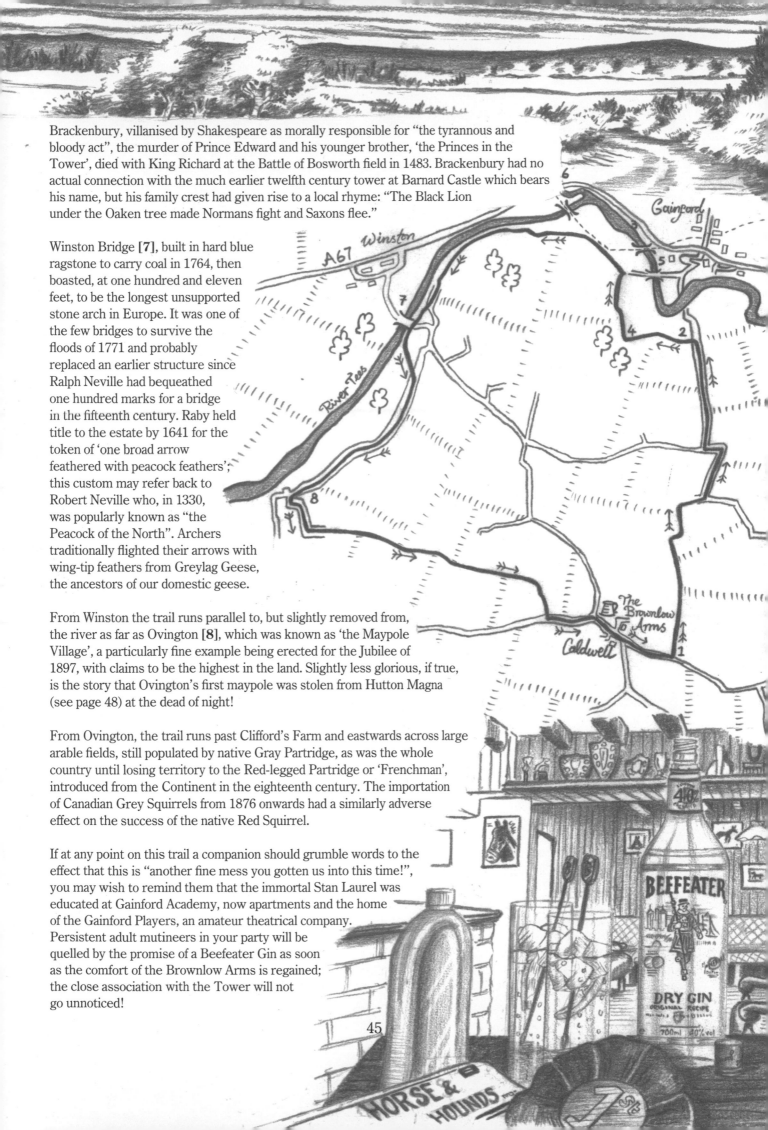

Brackenbury, villanised by Shakespeare as morally responsible for "the tyrannous and bloody act", the murder of Prince Edward and his younger brother, 'the Princes in the Tower', died with King Richard at the Battle of Bosworth field in 1483. Brackenbury had no actual connection with the much earlier twelfth century tower at Barnard Castle which bears his name, but his family crest had given rise to a local rhyme: "The Black Lion under the Oaken tree made Normans fight and Saxons flee."

Winston Bridge [7], built in hard blue ragstone to carry coal in 1764, then boasted, at one hundred and eleven feet, to be the longest unsupported stone arch in Europe. It was one of the few bridges to survive the floods of 1771 and probably replaced an earlier structure since Ralph Neville had bequeathed one hundred marks for a bridge in the fifteenth century. Raby held title to the estate by 1641 for the token of 'one broad arrow feathered with peacock feathers'; this custom may refer back to Robert Neville who, in 1330, was popularly known as "the Peacock of the North". Archers traditionally flighted their arrows with wing-tip feathers from Greylag Geese, the ancestors of our domestic geese.

From Winston the trail runs parallel to, but slightly removed from, the river as far as Ovington [8], which was known as 'the Maypole Village', a particularly fine example being erected for the Jubilee of 1897, with claims to be the highest in the land. Slightly less glorious, if true, is the story that Ovington's first maypole was stolen from Hutton Magna (see page 48) at the dead of night!

From Ovington, the trail runs past Clifford's Farm and eastwards across large arable fields, still populated by native Gray Partridge, as was the whole country until losing territory to the Red-legged Partridge or 'Frenchman', introduced from the Continent in the eighteenth century. The importation of Canadian Grey Squirrels from 1876 onwards had a similarly adverse effect on the success of the native Red Squirrel.

If at any point on this trail a companion should grumble words to the effect that this is "another fine mess you gotten us into this time!", you may wish to remind them that the immortal Stan Laurel was educated at Gainford Academy, now apartments and the home of the Gainford Players, an amateur theatrical company. Persistent adult mutineers in your party will be quelled by the promise of a Beefeater Gin as soon as the comfort of the Brownlow Arms is regained; the close association with the Tower will not go unnoticed!

The Squirrel's Tale

egend records that the oak tree, after which the village tavern in Hutton Magna is named, sprang up as a sapling on the green, not as the result of some random accident of nature, but as a consequence of a judgement delivered by a wise and far sighted owl, on two families of cantankerous squirrels.

One Autumn night, in the times when men still feared the wrath of dragons and it was by no means uncommon to hear of elves stealing buns from the bakers oven, at the height of a fierce thunderstorm, a bolt of lightning had struck the ancient oak tree on the village green.

The tree, rooted in the distant past, was known to all the creatures as Semoren 'the giver of good things'. His broad limbs shaded the grass and stout trunk sheltered all manner of creatures, and his acorns had sustained two families of red squirrels throughout many a long, bleak winter month.

The shock that cleft the mighty tree in twain similarly divided the two families of squirrels. Previously, in times of plenty, they had lived in harmony, sharing the bounty provided by the tree. Immediately, however, that hardship threatened, both families laid noisy claim to the half of the oak still left standing.

The owl, whose home was in a hollow in a part the trunk still left standing, knew that Semoren had suffered a mortal blow and would soon cease to afford shelter or food to any creature, save the grubs and boring insects which thrive on dead and dying timber. He summoned the leaders of both the squirrel clans before him, listened patiently as the animals squabbled and bickered, than he raised his wing to quiet them all.

"This noble tree has sustained our ancestors since the dawn of memory, yet Semoren has neither son nor daughter to replace him and, within a few short seasons, will provide for us no longer. If you consider only what you will eat today, you may go hungry tomorrow and neither shall my sons nor their sons enjoy shelter from the wind and rain".

The wise owl bade the squirrels collect all the ripe acorns and to divide them into three equal piles.

One each he gave to the two squirrel leaders to sustain their families. The third pile he scattered upon the green, decreeing that no animal should disturb the acorns where they fell and that, when one might germinate, sending roots into the soil and leaves towards the sky, no creature would nibble at its foliage or strip its bark.

So it came to pass that a fine new oak tree sprang from the ground and the creatures called the tree The Daughter of Semoren. Harmony returned to the community. Generations passed, the village, once called Hutton Longvillers, became Hutton Magna and the tale was passed down the years lest the wisdom of the owl should be lost and the creatures should forfeit their home again.

The village grew, people multiplied, and the country fought battles upon the seas. Everywhere oak trees were felled to build houses, men-of-war and to provide roof props for the lead mines.

The Daughter of Semoren was not spared; felled one spring morning. Henceforward, there were no acorns to collect, no wise owl to advise and the creatures fled in fear and confusion, leaving the tavern to bear silent witness to the past.

Even now, on a moonlit night you may hear an owl's haunting cry by the Oak Tree Inn, calling for man to replace what he has taken and to remind the creatures that, should man destroy himself eventually, the animals might still recover the ways of their ancestors and live in harmony again would they but remember to share and to exercise prudence with Nature's gifts.

47

The squirrel's domain.

(5 miles, 8 kilometers, easy walking.)

On November 18th, 1935, the entire estate comprising Hutton Magna, Ovington and Wycliffe was offered at public auction on the instructions of Lt. Colonel Walter George Raleigh Chichester-Constable. The Oak Tree Inn was sold to its present owners for seven hundred pounds, the tenant at the time being a Mrs. Snailham, who paid the annual rent of £ 28-10-0. Turning right from the door of the Oak Tree, head southwards, following the road to the end of the village, around a sharp right hand bend. At the next sharp corner [1], where the road turns southwards, our trail heads due north before turning west, just after the path crosses Hutton Beck [2], a tributary stream of the River Tees.

River catchments are the physical area drained by a single river system and, because they are usually dominated by the main river, the importance of the tributaries is frequently overlooked. From the merest seasonal trickle, just as veins are as vital as each artery to the human body, streams matter to the health of the river system as a whole. A clear example of this can be seen from the mitigating effects of the feeder streams after the Tees pollution of 1983 (see page 12).

The tributaries, unaffected by the spillage, were Nature's insurance against disaster, holding stocks of genetically true young with which to recolonise the main flow. Many fish species and invertebrates spawn in tiny streams each with their own variation on the catchments genetic identity. The effects of stocking fish from other rivers and fish farms may cause long term damage and are little understood (see page 12).

The trail describes several 'dog legs' to arrive at Whorlton Bridge [3] (see page 37) and the Lido, along whose river bank the trail turns eastwards to the site of the old cable ferry station, abandoned after the bridge was built. The ruins of the boat house and the remains of the treacherously steep steps on the far bank are still visible and there is a local tradition that a 'tap' room stood close to the water's edge. Called the Boot and Shoe, it dispensed 'Dutch courage' to nervous passengers and more than one of its customers were reputed to have fallen into the river after a good session at the ale.

A few hundred yards further down stream, the trail passes the site of the ancient animal ford, which, moderate river flows allowing, could be waded by strings of packhorses, oxen and cattle. There is no telling how many men and beasts have perished whilst using the various fords and stepping stone crossings over the river. The 'Tees Roll' (see page 16), a wall of water often twelve or more feet in height could sweep downstream without any warning. In the 1920's, one young amateur photograher choosing a 'head on' picture for her album, was consumed instantly by the Roll which travelled downstream at some twenty miles an hour.

The building of reservoirs, and particularly Cow Green (see page 21), has virtually eliminated this phenomenon, none the less a healthy respect for the fickle and volatile nature of the Tees is recommended to those who wish to become veteran photographers, and, if you felt moved by the mighty power of water to sing the first verse of Hymn 487, Ancient and Modern, you really could not have picked a more appropriate spot.

Wycliffe [4] reasonably claims to be the birth place of John Wyclif (1324 - 1384), "the Morning Star of the Reformation". His father was Lord of the Manor of Wycliffe, the family retaining the title until 1611, and his brother its parson. However, it was to John that history was kind, being, thanks to the protection of John of Gaunt, one of the few heretics who challenged the teaching of Rome yet died of natural causes in his own bed.

Wyclif was an Oxford scholar and progressive thinker. His followers, contemptuously referred to as Lollards (literally: 'mumblers and mutterers') who were many and loyal, wrote the first full translation of the whole bible into English. The Latin text was used and the result was clumsy and too literal for most tastes. The translation was soon revised by others using the original Greek and Hebrew versions, none the less, this first work is considered to have signalled the birth of modern English literature.

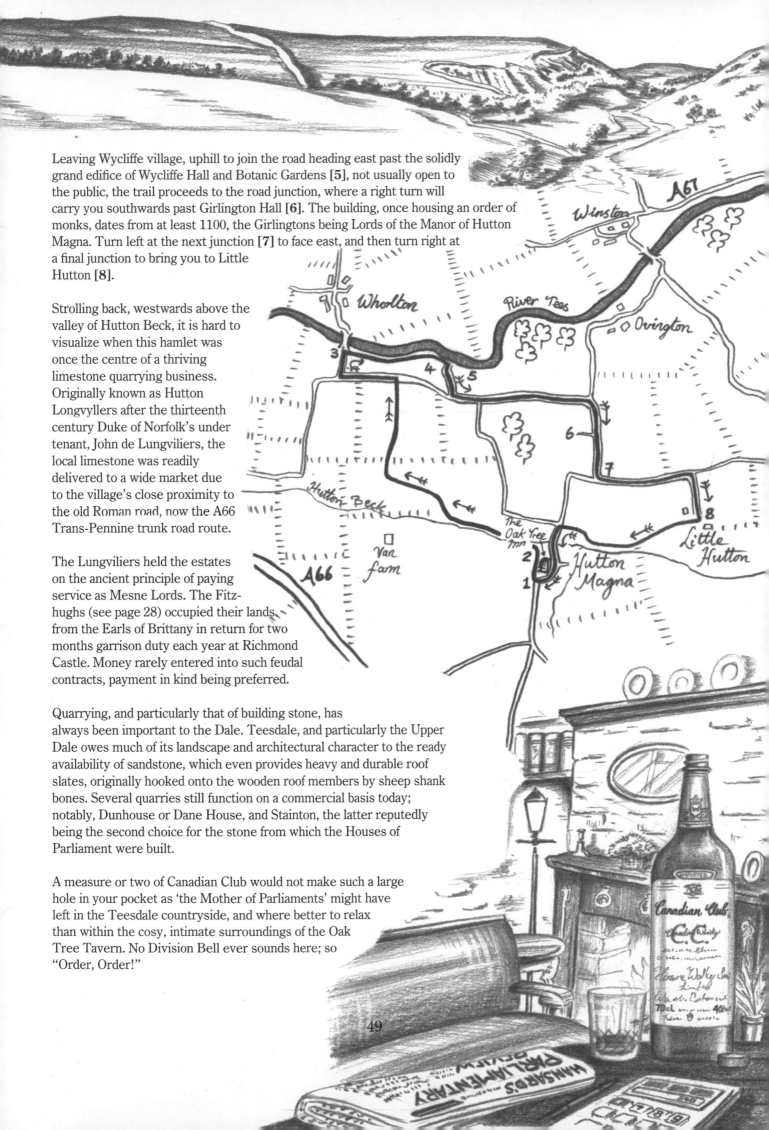

Leaving Wycliffe village, uphill to join the road heading east past the solidly grand edifice of Wycliffe Hall and Botanic Gardens [5], not usually open to the public, the trail proceeds to the road junction, where a right turn will carry you southwards past Girlington Hall [6]. The building, once housing an order of monks, dates from at least 1100, the Girlingtons being Lords of the Manor of Hutton Magna. Turn left at the next junction [7] to face east, and then turn right at a final junction to bring you to Little Hutton [8].

Strolling back, westwards above the valley of Hutton Beck, it is hard to visualize when this hamlet was once the centre of a thriving limestone quarrying business. Originally known as Hutton Longvyllers after the thirteenth century Duke of Norfolk's under tenant, John de Lungviliers, the local limestone was readily delivered to a wide market due to the village's close proximity to the old Roman road, now the A66 Trans-Pennine trunk road route.

The Lungviliers held the estates on the ancient principle of paying service as Mesne Lords. The Fitz-hughs (see page 28) occupied their lands from the Earls of Brittany in return for two months garrison duty each year at Richmond Castle. Money rarely entered into such feudal contracts, payment in kind being preferred.

Quarrying, and particularly that of building stone, has always been important to the Dale. Teesdale, and particularly the Upper Dale owes much of its landscape and architectural character to the ready availability of sandstone, which even provides heavy and durable roof slates, originally hooked onto the wooden roof members by sheep shank bones. Several quarries still function on a commercial basis today; notably, Dunhouse or Dane House, and Stainton, the latter reputedly being the second choice for the stone from which the Houses of Parliament were built.

A measure or two of Canadian Club would not make such a large hole in your pocket as 'the Mother of Parliaments' might have left in the Teesdale countryside, and where better to relax than within the cosy, intimate surroundings of the Oak Tree Tavern. No Division Bell ever sounds here; so "Order, Order!"

THE HARE'S TALE

In the times when rabble armies pillaged the Northern Lands, burning farms and sometimes whole villages and towns, here lived in a simple croft, where now stands the Raby Moor Inn, a comely maiden of mild and gentle manner. Such was her virtue that, despite her humble origin, she had won the heart of a wealthy squire and the couple were betrothed to be wed that year as soon as the harvest should be safely gathered in.

The Squire's sisters were jealous of the maiden and told her that she was plain to behold and that their brother would soon tire of her once they were wed. So vexed was she that sleep abandoned her and she took to wandering in the meadows behind her home to the light of the pale moon above.

On the third night of her solitary vigil, as the hour passed midnight, the maiden heard a muted cry from within a bramble thicket. There she found a hare, caught fast in the dense tangle and, forgetting her sorrow for a moment, ignoring the sharp cruelty of the thorns, set herself straightway to freeing the ensnared beast which trembled all the while with fear.

Thus unentangled, the hare, panting heavily, did not lope away but sat upon the grass until his deep sobbing breaths subsided, and then he spoke, "Gentle girl child of Man, for your kindness one wish may I grant you". The maiden pondered awhile whilst stroking the long soft ears of the mystical animal.

"I wish that you would make me more beautiful than the fabled Helen of Troy; that I may never become a burden to the soul of my beloved". Now was it the hare's turn to ponder and he cautioned her urgently to reconsider the nature of her wish, since such beauty alone might bring in its train more danger than reward.

The maiden, thinking only of her lover's pleasure, insisted and the hare rose from his haunches, slipped a small draw-string bag around his neck, and sped up into the vast canopy of bright stars.

50

The maiden watched the celestial
progress entranced as the hare, cleaving a glowing meteoric trail,
raced from star to star, describing orbits around the planets and flicking the waning Moon with
his powerful hind legs, causing it to spin awhile, alarming learned astronomers in the Orient.

The hare rested again beside the Maiden, bade her slip off her simple gown and lie outstretched
upon the moonlit meadow made moist by the fall of dew. Dipping his paw into the pouch he
sprinkled her with a dazzling veil of stardust, freshly gathered from the heavens.

When she arose she was clad in silks and pearls, her eyes shone with pure sapphire, hair
glossed blacker than the raven's wing, soft skin paler than the finest alabaster, her form was
faultless and her graceful motion serenity itself.

The fame of her beauty spread faster than the flame of a tinder dry heather fire on the high
summer moors. Soon came the King and, upon the instant, he decreed her his. The squire
protested and the King ordered him forthwith, that very evening, to fight a duel of mortal
combat with his champion, the maiden to be the prize.

Bravely though the squire fought he fell before his monarch, who spoke thus to the maiden,
"This night, beckoned now by the stealthy gathering dusk, is the shortest of Our year. You may
rest these brief hours with your family 'till dawn graces Our Eastern skies; thereafter thou shall
be Our queen and shall attend Our court and bedchamber".

Once night had fallen, the distraught maiden slipped away unnoticed to the meadow where she
cried out in deep despair until the hare came once again to sit by her side. "Although your wish
was foolish it was unselfishly made," he sighed and told her what might yet be done that night.
She nodded silently as if to say, "Mystical hare, you have proved to be wiser than I and I shall
do your bidding".

Six long tresses of her hair cut he and plaitted them to form a circle. Six tears of pure sorrow
caught he and dropped them within the ring of lusterous black. Straightway the hare
and maiden flew together through the dawning sky. Pausing momentarily to catch
the spirit of the squire, lingering alone on the margin of the firmament, all three
ascended the while to join a great constellation, and there to be content.

Now, if legend you will believe, should the Summer Solstice fall upon a
cloudless night in Teesdale, and should you search the sky with care, you
might recognize the bright star the lovers made their own and occasionally
you might glimpse a streak of light leaping from horizon to horizon as the
hare dares time stand still.

the hare's lope.

(4 miles, 6.5 kilometers, easy walking.)

Leave the Raby Moor and the hamlet of Burnthouses heading north as a border raider might have done, in the 1030's, when King Canute may have held court at Raby, the Bulmer Tower reputedly standing on the site of his castle. The Norse word 'rey' meant border and it is possible that the Roman road linking the Rey Cross on Stainmore and running past Raby northwards to Dere Street south of Binchester may have been part of the Anglo-Scottish border. For eighteen years from 1139, when King Stephen ceded the Earldom of Northumbria to the Scots, the River Tees was, arguably, the boundary, a situation rectified by his successor, King Henry II.

Entering Cockfield from the south, the subject of borders may still be on your mind and it would not be at all inappropriate if you marched into the village whistling "Dixie" because it was here that the remarkable family of Dixons lived. Descended from a former steward of Raby Castle, the family prospered, acquiring extensive interests in the coal-fields which surrounded Cockfield.

Their wealth allowed for education and the time with which to pursue their various interests. George Dixon, born in 1731, discovered the first method of extracting a flammable gas from coal (see page 16), whilst his brother Jerimiah, an accomplished astronomer and mathematician, journeyed to America. There with Charles Mason, between 1763 - 67, he surveyed the 'Mason-Dixon' line separating Maryland from Pennsylvania and, later, the Confederate South, 'Dixie' from the Unionist North, two sides destined to fight the Civil War of 1861.

Much closer to home, a third brother, John, mathematician and surveyor, prepared the maps in 1796 which would enable the enclosure, by Act of Parliament, of Barnard Castle Moor in Marwood, the Town Fields being enclosed in 1783 and 1794. By coincidence, Cockfield Fell [1], the six hundred acres of common land on your left as you progress eastwards through the village, escaped enclosure. To this day local persons are appointed as 'Fell Reeves' to apportion grazing, space for pigeon lofts and access to opencast coal among the residents. The Fell, containing a wealth of industrial heritage, was listed as an ancient monument in 1974.

Standing near to the western margin of the coal and sandstone bearing Carboniferous Shales, Cockfield has been inhabited, and the shallow coal-seams worked since pre-Roman times. Sub-surface deposits were, similarly to lead, accessed by 'bell pits' or vertical shafts dug down to the seam, allowing limited lateral extraction before the danger of roof collapse forced the miners to abandon the workings and to sink another pit a short distance further along the line of the seam. The spoil from the new pit would partly fill the old shaft, leaving the characteristic dish shaped deformations all over the hillside.

At the cross roads [2], the trail cuts back in a north-westerly direction across the Fell to run upstream on the right bank of the River Gaunless, crossing the track bed of the old Barnard Castle to Bishop Auckland Railway. Across the valley lies the bed of the Butterknowle to Haggerleases branch line (see Page 32), a network of tramways fed the station by the Slack.

Take a short diversion to see George Dixon's Skew Arch Railway Bridge [3] and consider the importance of coal to the later history of County Durham. In 1800, nine thousand men extracted two million tons, but by 1913, over one hundred and sixty five thousand men were extracting forty one and a half million tons, coal displacing agriculture as the major employer and wealth provider.

The main market was London, whose fortunes and growth were heavily reliant on the steady flow of colliers from the North East ports. Remarkably, the natural landscape of County Durham has been restored, the pit heaps, slag piles and other scars reclaimed forever.

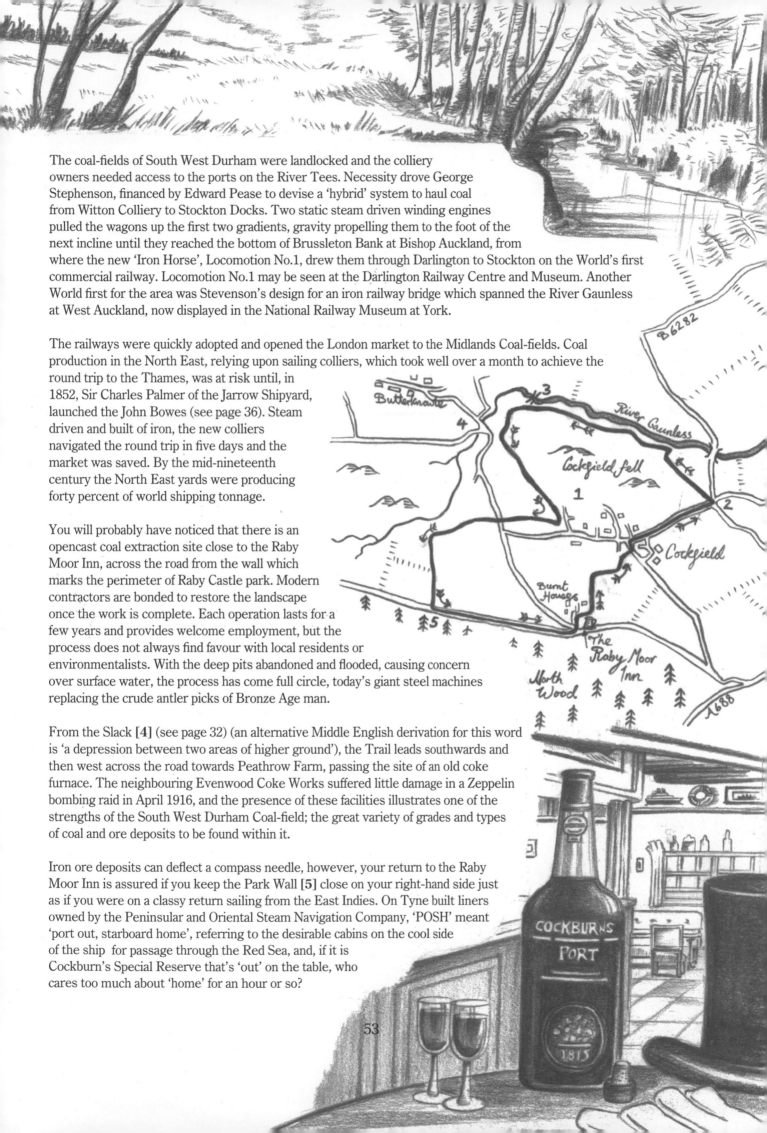

The coal-fields of South West Durham were landlocked and the colliery owners needed access to the ports on the River Tees. Necessity drove George Stephenson, financed by Edward Pease to devise a 'hybrid' system to haul coal from Witton Colliery to Stockton Docks. Two static steam driven winding engines pulled the wagons up the first two gradients, gravity propelling them to the foot of the next incline until they reached the bottom of Brussleton Bank at Bishop Auckland, from where the new 'Iron Horse', Locomotion No.1, drew them through Darlington to Stockton on the World's first commercial railway. Locomotion No.1 may be seen at the Darlington Railway Centre and Museum. Another World first for the area was Stevenson's design for an iron railway bridge which spanned the River Gaunless at West Auckland, now displayed in the National Railway Museum at York.

The railways were quickly adopted and opened the London market to the Midlands Coal-fields. Coal production in the North East, relying upon sailing colliers, which took well over a month to achieve the round trip to the Thames, was at risk until, in 1852, Sir Charles Palmer of the Jarrow Shipyard, launched the John Bowes (see page 36). Steam driven and built of iron, the new colliers navigated the round trip in five days and the market was saved. By the mid-nineteenth century the North East yards were producing forty percent of world shipping tonnage.

You will probably have noticed that there is an opencast coal extraction site close to the Raby Moor Inn, across the road from the wall which marks the perimeter of Raby Castle park. Modern contractors are bonded to restore the landscape once the work is complete. Each operation lasts for a few years and provides welcome employment, but the process does not always find favour with local residents or environmentalists. With the deep pits abandoned and flooded, causing concern over surface water, the process has come full circle, today's giant steel machines replacing the crude antler picks of Bronze Age man.

From the Slack [4] (see page 32) (an alternative Middle English derivation for this word is 'a depression between two areas of higher ground'), the Trail leads southwards and then west across the road towards Peathrow Farm, passing the site of an old coke furnace. The neighbouring Evenwood Coke Works suffered little damage in a Zeppelin bombing raid in April 1916, and the presence of these facilities illustrates one of the strengths of the South West Durham Coal-field; the great variety of grades and types of coal and ore deposits to be found within it.

Iron ore deposits can deflect a compass needle, however, your return to the Raby Moor Inn is assured if you keep the Park Wall [5] close on your right-hand side just as if you were on a classy return sailing from the East Indies. On Tyne built liners owned by the Peninsular and Oriental Steam Navigation Company, 'POSH' meant 'port out, starboard home', referring to the desirable cabins on the cool side of the ship for passage through the Red Sea, and, if it is Cockburn's Special Reserve that's 'out' on the table, who cares too much about 'home' for an hour or so?

A TEESDALE TREAT - 'THE MENU'...

500 million years B.C. Formation of Palaezoic Silurian Slates, now the oldest elements of the Teesdale landscape.

370 million years B.C. Deposition of Lower Carboniferous Limestones and Upper Carboniferous Millstone Grit series.

290 million years B.C. Igneous quartz dolomite extrusions of Whin-Sill during Armorican-Hercynian period of mountain building. Heating mineralises Carboniferous rocks producing commercial quantities of lead ore, dolerite and barytes etc.

8,000 - 10,000 B.C. End of last ice age, (The Quaternary) glaciers retreat, leaving boulder clay and morainic debris.

6,000 B.C. Stone age man hunts in Forest of Teesdale.

2,000 B.C. Bronze Age settlements appear.

850 B.C. Iron Age settlements and industry established.

43 A.D. Roman influence begins under Emperor Claudius.

80 Roman Legions engage the Brigantes on Stainmore.

122 - 127 Hadrian's Wall built to control Picts and Scots.

200 6th Legion stationed at Greta Bridge and Bowes.

400 Bowes Camp the last outpost to be abandoned by retreating Romans. Scots and West Saxon invasions.

598 Saxon victory at Catterick establishes Northern Kingdoms.

627 Paulinus of York baptizes Edwin, King of Northumbria.700 Lindisfarne gospel written.

730 Death of Venerable Bede of Jarrow.

793 Lindisfarne sacked, Viking invasions begin.

882 Followers of St. Cuthbert granted lands between the Rivers Tyne and Tees, "The Land of the Prince Bishops".

954 Eric Bloodaxe, last King of the Viking Yorvic empire, centered on York, murdered on Stainmore by Earl Maccus.

1016 Canute becomes King of Norway, Denmark and England and adopts the style "Emperor of the North".

1066 William, Duke of Normandy begins Norman Conquest.

1070 "The Harrying of the North" by the Normans, land laid waste. Battle of Hunderthwaite, where the Scottish King Malcolm Canmore slew many English noblemen.

1086 Doomsday Book records wealth south of the River Tees.

1092 William Rufus grants Barnard Castle to Guy de Baliol. Rey Cross on Stainmore, "The Cross of Kings", ceases to mark the ancient boundary between England and Scotland.

1109 First recorded fortification of Barnard Castle.

1170 Bowes Castle built by Alan Nigar, Count of Brittany.

1178 Bernard Baliol grants borough charter to Barnard Castle.

1180 The Boldron Book, Bishop Hugh de Puiset's equivalent of Doomsday Book, records wealth and lands north of Tees.

1195 Eggleston Abbey founded by the White Cannons.

1201 Fitz-hughs, the Lords of Romaldkirk, build a castle on the Hagg at Cotherstone, which is soon destroyed by Scots.

1282 John Baliol's widow, Devorguilla of Galloway endows Baliol Collage, Oxford, and Sweetheart Abbey, Dumfries.

1296 King Edward I bestows crown of Scotland on John Baliol's son, also called John. The two kings quarreled, John exiled to Bailleul, the original Baliol family estate in Picardy.

1330 Raby Castle begins to be built in today's form.

1335 County Bridge built at Barnard Castle to replace Roman ford which had linked their forts at Bowes and Binchester.

1340 Bowes Castle abandoned, badly damaged by the Scots.

1350 The Black Death, 'Prima Pestilentia' ravages the Dale.

1421 Lead mining activity in Teesdale first chronicled.

1450 Bowes family build Streatlam Castle.

1470 Mortham Tower built by Rokebys as a pele tower.

1471 Richard Neville, "Warwick the King Maker" killed at Battle of Barnet. Barnard Castle reverts to the Crown.

1485 Battle of Bosworth Field, Richard III killed.

1536 Dissolution of the monasteries begins and the Pilgrimage of Grace by the Northern Catholic rebels suppressed. Egglestone Abbey abandoned.

1569 Rising of the North led by Percys and Nevilles; Earls of Northumberland and Westmorland. Barnard Castle held for Queen Elizabeth I by Sir George Bowes for eleven vital days. Nevilles forfeit Raby Castle, lands seized by the Crown.

1636 Bamard Castle in a derelict state, demolished by Sir Henry Vane who took the stone to improve Raby Castle.

1637 Vane, a Crown Trustee, buys the Raby Estates.

1644 Battle of Marsdon Moor, Rokebys, Royalists, stripped of Mortham Tower and lands, bought by Robinson family.

1645 & 1648 Raby Castle besieged by Royalists.

1648 Oliver Cromwell visits Barnard Castle.

1660 Bowes family acquires land south of the River Tees.

1662 Vane the Younger beheaded for supporting Cromwell, however, the family allowed to retain the Raby estates.

1665 The Great Plague decimates Teesdale population.

1704 Wynch Bridge suspended across Tees near Holwick.

1735 Rokeby built by Sir Thomas Robinson, "Long Sir Tom".

1747 Market Cross built in Barnard Castle, as town hall.

1753 George Dixon abstracts flammable gas from coal.

1760 London Lead Mining Co. arrives in Middleton.

1763-7 Jerimiah Dixon of Cockfield surveys Mason-Dixon Line between Virginia and Pennsylvania, birth of 'Dixie'.

1765 John Wesley deluged by Barnard Castle fire engine.

1769 Morritts buy Rokeby from the Robinson family.

1771 The great flood of the Tees.

1773 Eggleston Abbey Toll Bridge built, funded by J. Morritt.

1802 Wynch Bridge collapses.

1811 Middleton bridge re-built after initial disaster.

1813 Scott's epic poem, "Rokeby" published.

1815 London Lead Mining Co. begins to build in Middleton.

1829 Whorlton ferry replaced by a suspension bridge.

1835 Charles Dickens researches school life in Teesdale.

1836 Palatinate of the See of Durham restored to Crown.

1854 Witham Hall built in Barnard Castle.

1861 Trans-Pennine Railway opened to Kirby Stephen.

1868 Tees Valley Railway opened to Middleton.

1877 Bainbridge memorial fountain erected in Middleton.

1880 Middleton house H.Q. for London Lead Mining Co.

1886 Whin-Sill quarries opened in the Upper Dale.

1891 Richard Watson, poet, dies due to an accident whilst building Holwick Mansion for Cosmo Bonsor M.P.

1892 Bowes Museum opens. John and Josephine both dead.

1905 London Lead Mining Co. bankrupt due to the low prices of foreign ore, quits Middleton. Small scale mining continues.

1914-1918 First World War. Zeppelin bombs Evenwood .

1920 Pollution stops salmon and sea trout running the Tees.

1927 Hamsterly Forest planted.

1939-1945 Second World War. Glaxo penicillin factory open.

1959 Remains of Streatlam Castle demolished.

1963 Much of Upper Dale designated as nature reserve.

1965 Tees Valley Railway lines closed.

1967 Work begins on Cow Green Reservoir.

1987 Upper dale designated as an A.O.N.B.

1995 Tees Barrage built at Stockton, salmon runs returning.

THE BRIDGE INN,
MIDDLETON·IN·TEESDALE

55

...A Chilling Ghoulish Soup!...

The bare, dusty dry skeleton of a chronology, an anonymous compendium of historical dates, can sometimes deny the fascinating detail of the human aspects of history which, if known, will at once, put flesh upon the bones and stimulate a flow of myth and legend sufficient to animate the slumbering creature of times past.

Ironies abound in the story of Teesdale, for who might think that it would be safer to stand upon a collapsing bridge, rather than by its side? In fact, of the eleven haymakers crossing the original Wynch Bridge, close to Holwick village, "A restless gangway to which few strangers dare trust themselves", when it collapsed on August 20th 1802, only John Bainbridge of Howgill perished. Not so fortunate some nine years later was the local butcher, Richard Attee, and his wife, who stood marvelling at the structural faults in the nearly completed bridge at Middleton when it collapsed suddenly burying both in the rubble.

The spirits of these unfortunate victims of accident do not seem to have swollen the ranks of the many others that are variously reputed to roam the Dale from the Meeting of the Waters and beyond, right up the valley to Cauldron Snout, where the Singing Lady still sits atop the foaming cataract. Jilted by her lover, a feckless lead miner, she had cast her mortal body from the summit to perish in the foaming torrent below.

Not far downstream, close by Holwick, is the site of one of the many ancient, abandoned villages of the Dale, Unthank, where the Weird Hairy Bairn, "Dubskelpie", of distant legend still roams the hills with the spirit of William Robinson, a simple shepherd, murdered on the 8th of April 1794 on Holwick Fell by person or persons unknown - or was this foul deed the work of the Hairy Bairn itself? Perhaps, on moonlit nights, as some folk say, they meet in Fairy Dell, hidden in the hillside, on the fell just south of the strangely named Hungry Hall.

The last Fitz-hugh, Lord of Romaldkirk, met his sudden end whilst pursuing a white hart from Marwood Chase. The deer lured the horse and rider, separated from the main hunting party by the speed of the chase, to the very edge of a high cliff known as Percymire Castle, where upon it vanished and the huntsman and his steed plunged on and into the "awful dell" below, and there to perish in the rock strewn river bed.

Watery graves have fuelled strange superstitions such as that surrounding Peg Powler, a green haired sprite with an eye for a young child, manifested by her 'suds' and 'cream', the frothy sponges and slicks which sometimes appear on the surface of the Tees. Legend does not relate, however, whether Peg's victims and the spirit of Lord Fitz-hugh suffered the same ultimate fate as the Mortham Dobbie, the ghost of a serving maid wronged by one of the Lords of Rokeby and persuaded by the Latin verses of a priest to dwell under the Dairy Bridge, until both bridge and spirit were swept away in the great flood of 1771.

Incantations of a wholly different sort, "Let those who sleep, sleep; those who are awake, be awake" were required to extract the magic potential from an extraordinary artifact, "the Hand of Glory". The mummified hand of an executed criminal, grasping a candle made from his own tallow could, when lit, induce profound sleep. The only recorded attempt to use this sorcery in Teesdale, at Old Spital, Stainmore in 1797, ended in abject failure for the would be perpetrators when a serving girl doused the 'candle' with a pitcher of milk.

Skinny felons would make poor candles; perhaps folk lore should have included swine such as the Felon Sow of Rokeby, "The grisliest beast that ere might bee", owned by Ralph of Rokeby and judiciously donated by him to the Friars of Richmond. Two friars were repulsed by the beast; swords broken and much bruised, they fled home. Only after a further epic struggle, lasting most of the next day, did two more vanquish the fiercesome sow, whose carcass was carried back in triumph, prompting the friars to celebrate by singing a merry Te Deum.

Ironic too that an eccentric nineteenth century recluse, dressed in monks habit and living in the ruins of the Round Tower of Barnard Castle, should have been evicted from his chosen lodgings, all be it temporarily, for pretending to be a ghost and thereby frightening visitors; a clear case of "carrying coals to Newcastle"!

THE OAK TREE INN,
HUTTON MAGNA

57

…SOME SAVOURY MORSELS…

The lack of hurricanes in the Home Counties as reported by Henry Higgins in 'My Fair Lady', conveniently ignores the ferocity of the Helm Wind which can render the Beaufort Scale quite redundant. This occasional meteorological phenomenon, technically described as Katabatic, strikes Fiends' Fell, at the very top of Teesdale, with sufficient force to flatten everything in its path. In the seventh century it attracted the attention of St. Paulinus, flush from the triumph of baptising King Edwin, and seeking new challenges and conversions. Legend relates that the Saint failed to quell the fiends, but left a cross to mark his ascent of the 2,930 ft (893m) summit, the second highest in England after Scarfell, and the bleak spot was renamed Cross Fell accordingly. The Tees is born and assumes its tempestuous nature from this place, the South Tyne rising close by to the west.

Jumping to the Eastern boundary of the Dale, the religious theme continues with the coincidental sequence which befell the aptly named Rev. John Cranke of Gainford who, in 1814, married J. Pigg on the Saturday, christened H.Lamb on the Sunday and buried J. Hogg on the following Monday.

Lists of names with humourous connotations are often associated with school roles, however, in 1837, Charles Dickens found little amusing in the conditions prevailing at Mr. Shaw's academy 'The Villa' at Bowes. The conditions in all four such establishments in the village were exposed and possibly expanded upon in 'Nicholas Nickleby'. The book earned Dickens several thousand pounds and the student population of Bowes contracted.

Similarly harsh conditions prevailed at Woden Croft, near Cotherstone, where Richard Cobden, a great reformer of his day, received some of his education. A century earlier Alexander Pope had written, "'Tis education forms the common mind: Just as the twig is bent the tree's inclined." This 'twig', in later life a founder of the Anti-Corn Law League, addressed a crowd on the subject of the landed gentry thus: "They not only cling to feudal abuses, but they actually try to put a restraint upon the supply of food to the people." The same comments might have applied equally well to the governors of these 'educational establishments'.

Cotherstone, thus named because it lay a somewhat unsubstantiated claim to be one of the many temporary resting places for the mortal remains of St. Cuthbert, carried for seven long years by his followers after their eviction from Lindisfarne in the late eighth century, was by the late eighteenth century a devoutly Quaker community. So ardently did the dwellers follow their beliefs that their piety was recorded by the less reverent in a local rhyme; "Cotherstone where they christen't cauves, hoppled lops and knee-banded spiders".

St Cuthbert's earthly remains may have covered many miles in seven years wandering, but the Teesdale Relics' All Comers Record for Distance in a Single Journey, may well be held by the heart of John Baliol the Elder. After his death, his wife Devorguilla, kept this vital organ in an ivory casket which never left her side; widow and heart were buried together at Sweetheart Abbey, Dumfries, a foundation endowed by her in 1273.

Earthy remains of a more common sort used to exercise the minds of simple folk. In ancient times, the "fruits of Natur's great bounty", left by livestock were of great value in fertilising the strip fields; indeed, Lords of the Manor would insist on all stock overnighting on their fields. The peasants of Barnard Castle, early ancestors of today's rose growing enthusiasts, used to thwart this instruction with bucket and shovel at the dead of night.

Subterfuge was by no means the preserve of the peasant classes. In the mid-sixteenth century, when, after the Rising of the North, Raby Castle was confiscated from the Nevilles, Sir Henry Vane, a Crown Trustee desirous of acquiring it and its estates for himself, described the Castle to Charles I as; a "hurrock of staines." Later, whilst staying at Raby the King commented; "Ca' ye that a hurrock o' staines? By my faith, I ha' na' sic anither hurrock in a' my realm!" Not long afterwards, King Charles I was beheaded, despite Vane's pleas for clemency, but the "hurrock o' staines" still stands today as a magnificently preserved monument to history.

Apocryphal tales populate Teesdale as thickly as 'hoppled lops' on a cat's ear. Returning to the top of the dale, to Harewood, where, a road having been built finally, MacAdam visited his work in the first four wheeled carriage ever seen in those remote parts. The entire population chased it crying out; "Darra, Lad, d'girt wheil's gaun t'overtak t'littleun." No doubt the Dale has played host to a few 'shaggy dogs' in its time too!

THE KINGS HEAD,
MIDDLETON-IN-TEESDALE

59

...The main course...

The Dale has resonated to the colourful clamour of the hunt for over eight thousand years, and whilst the methods of the Chase may have changed dramatically, from the tribal pursuit of a quarry on foot by Neolithic man, clad in skins and brandishing crude flint headed axes, to the deployment of superbly crafted sporting guns, thoroughbred gundogs and sharply tailored tweeds, the practical and social aspects of the hunt remained remarkably constant for hundreds of years.

The rituals and traditions associated with hunting developed to fulfill certain specific needs. They combined the practical necessity to provide a source of fresh meat in winter, the lack of root crops for forage requiring the Autumn slaughter and salting of the cattle herds, with an absorbing occupation to divert the attentions and energies of a warlike nobility, who chose to leave the more weighty issues largely to the men of the Church.

It is clear from contemporary chronicles that to do battle, though frequently bloody and fatal in its outcome, was viewed as something akin to a sport, a challenge, a test of skill as in William Somerville's, 'The Chase', "My hoarse-sounding horn invites thee to the Chase, the Sport of Kings, Image of War without its Guilt". The hunt taught the skills of strategy, organisation, discipline and horsemanship to complement the weapons training gained in tournaments and jousting, although both the Chase and the Lists could prove as fatal as war.

The importance of hunting from Norman times to this very day is evidenced, in part, by the large tracts of ground which have been reserved for its pursuit. Between the mid-thirteenth and late seventeenth centuries, Marwood Chase enclosed hundreds of acres to the west and north west of Barnard Castle, but this enclosure pales into insignificance when set against the size of the Forests of Lune and Teesdale.

The need to maintain a healthy, balanced population demanded conservation measures on a grand scale. In 1131 open forest grazing was banned from 11th November to 1st April. Friths, enclosures in the wildest parts of the forests, were reserved for the rearing of deer and every aspect such as the identification of the oldest hind in each herd was carefully managed. The size and the value of the deer herds may be judged by the fact that the severe snows of 1673, part of the Mini Ice Age, killed over four hundred red deer in The Forest of Teesdale.

Our knowledge of early hunting is greatly enhanced by contemporary accounts such as those of Count Gaston de Foix's, 'La Chasse' (1390), Edward Duke of York's, 'The Master of the Game' (1415) and Turberville's 'Booke of Hunting' (1576), however, it must be remembered that Caxton set up his first printing press in 1476 and books of any sort were a scarce and valuable commodity, almost as scarce as the ability to read itself.

These works do illustrate how the hierarchy of the quarry changed over time with the hare rising from a lowly rank to stand alongside the deer, whilst the fox fell to become vermin and how the grouse and partridge remained, for a long while, in the company of the rabbits as "beasts of the warren". These changes tend to reflect the increasing value placed upon the different natural skills of each quarry species to evade capture and begin to distance the Chase from a predominantly food gathering function to one placing more emphasis on the social aspect which tends to dominate the field today, encouraging Dr. Johnson to remark that; "Hunting was the labour of the savages in North America, but the amusement of the gentlemen of England".

In recent times William Whitelaw, now Lord Whitelaw, accidentally peppered his host, the late Joe Nickerson, and a beater on the grouse moors above Holwick. The Tabloid press enjoyed a 'field day' and produced such headlines as "Silly Willie Bags a Pair!" What headline might a similar late eleventh century newspaper, 'The News of the Known World', have concocted about King William Rufus (Rufus the Red) after he fell to an arrow, reputedly mistaken by an errant archer for a deer - "Rueful Rufus Gets the Point" perhaps?

Teesdale is fortunate indeed to enjoy an enviable range of country pursuits which include: game fishing in the River Tees and reservoirs, shooting over grouse moors and at lower altitudes. The management skills needed to perpetuate viable, healthy populations of all manner of species are as important to the local economy today as in the fifteenth century when the Duke of Gloucester, soon to be Richard III, hunted the Dale with his retinue. This is the tradition, the privilege and the responsibility proudly borne by successive generations.

THE OLD WELL INN,
BARNARD CASTLE

61

...A DELICE OF POETIC DELIGHTS...

Whilst it would be unthinkable for a valley as rich and abundant in all of Nature's gifts as Teesdale not to have attracted the aesthetic attentions of artists and literary figures of national and international acclaim, and indeed not to have bred some of its own, it is true to say that it is unique and quite remarkable for such a sparsely populated area, remote from the acknowledged cultural centres of Europe, to possess a museum and art gallery of international rank and reputation.

The John and Josephine Bowes Museum is an extraordinary, French Renaissance style building of singular grandeur, and, thankfully, far removed from the typically turgid municipal architecture of late nineteenth century English public buildings. The museum, its collections and the skill of display demonstrated by its staff are the envy of many a city let alone a tranquil and picturesque market town like Barnard Castle.

William Wordsworth, whose wife was born in the North East, immortalised the great power of the Nevilles in "The White Doe of Rylstone", describing the plotting of 'the Rising of the North' in the Baron's Hall at Raby;

> Seven hundred knights, retainers all
> Of Neville, at their master's call
> Had sate together in Raby Hall!
> Such strength that Earldom had of yore.

Richard Watson, 'The Bard of Teesdale', sometimes compared in style to Rabbie Burns, was not a poet of the first order, but his verse captures the essence of Nature and contains a certain dramatic power;

> I've dwelt in towns and on wild moors
> And curious sights I've seen.
> But still my heart clings to the dale
> Where Tees rolls to the sea,
> Compared with what I've seen I'll say
> The Teesdale hills for me.

Sir Walter Scott, much taken by the Italianate splendour of the Palladian villa of Rokeby, its park setting and the infectious enthusiasm of his host, wrote to a friend, "It is one of the most enviable places I have ever seen", and drew heavily upon the legend and folk lore of Teesdale whilst compiling his epic poem "Rokeby";

> Nor Tees alone in dawning bright
> Shall rush upon the ravished site
> But many a tributary stream
> Each from its own dark dell shall gleam.

More recently, in the 1930s, Margaret Walker, a resident of Barnard Castle, Scott's 'ravished site', wrote the following in her 'Present from Teesdale'; verses which in many ways typify the spontaneous affection with which local people view their surroundings and the wealth of attraction which enriches their daily life;

> You have loved my lonely splendour, and gush of mighty falls,
> You have loved the rugged grandeur of my grey old castle walls,
> You have loved my singing breezes, and you loved my rushing wind,
> You have loved to roam my moorlands, with man's dwellings far behind.

And where else to sit, to savour and to contemplate the literary and artistic riches which complement our valley but within a traditional tavern, where in the immortal words of William Shenston, the eighteenth century poet;

> Who'er has travele'd life's dull round, where'er his stages may have been
> May sigh to think he still has found the warmest welcome in an inn.

THE BRIDGE INN,
WHORLTON

...A TASTE - A THIRST FOR MORE.

Effecting an introduction between two strangers, the one with a tendency towards a natural shyness, the other often preoccupied with the cares of modern life is, by common consent, an undertaking fraught by potential disappointment for all concerned.

Our clear purpose in writing this book for you is to offer a glimpse, a highly selective taste, of just some of the absorbing interests and pleasures which are to be discovered in such abundance throughout Teesdale, and to hope that this introduction might lead to a warm friendship, or even blossom into a more passionate affair.

Each year, many people pay the valley the most cursory of visits, by car or coach, to marvel momentarily at the beauty of the land forms, colours and changing moods through a distorting veil of toughened glass, before driving on elsewhere, sampling fleeting impressions of other vistas, other blurred memories in a soon forgotten tour of somewhere.

This is not enough. It satisfies neither visitor nor visited. More should heed Lord Byron's words and not allow "Decay's effacing fingers" to "Have swept the lines where beauty lingers".

Teesdale deserves to be granted the courtesy of time, and especially so in this hurried age; to be felt, smelt, touched and known more tenderly and intimately. Stand, if you will, by her river's edge, listen to the flow, let your fingers caress the rounded stones and pebbles which litter the water's margin and, in their smoothness, sense the unhurried purpose in time's measured passing.

Lean, if you can spare one solitary moment, against a worn fragment of an ancient castle wall, feel the mellow stones, warmed by the last rays of the setting sun, and imagine the pageant of persons, events and change which has paraded before your chosen post.

Sit snugly, if you have a mind to relax, within the friendly tavern bar and know that you are part of a continuum, centuries old, steeped in humour and fellowship and be content that your company and your custom will be valued and will help sustain one of the best loved and most valued features of the Dale; the traditional Teesdale tavern.

"We wish you all God's speed upon your journeys."

THE STAG'S HEAD,
BUTTERKNOWLE

1
to Alston
2
RIVER TEES
HUDESHOPE BECK
to Stanhope
5
6
holwick
8
7
MIDDLETON-
IN-TEESDALE
15
14
12
13
EGGLESTON
BURN
EGGLESTON
18
LAITHKIRK
10
mickleton
17
RIVER LUNE
19
ROMALDKIRK
20
to BROUGH (m6)
9
RIVER t
hunderthw
3
RIVER BALDER
23
co
16
11
4
EDINBURGH
BERWICK
DEEPDA
GLASGOW
N
S
DUMFRIES
NEWCASTLE
NO
SE
CARLISLE
DURHAM
PENRITH
to M6 & LAKE DISTRICT
BARNARD
CASTLE
BELFAST
22 BOWES
KESWICK
YORK
21
ISLE O'MAN
PORT OF
HULL
LEEDS
IRISH
SEA
MANCHESTER

TEESDALE, CO. DURHAM

the visitor and to the sportsman alike

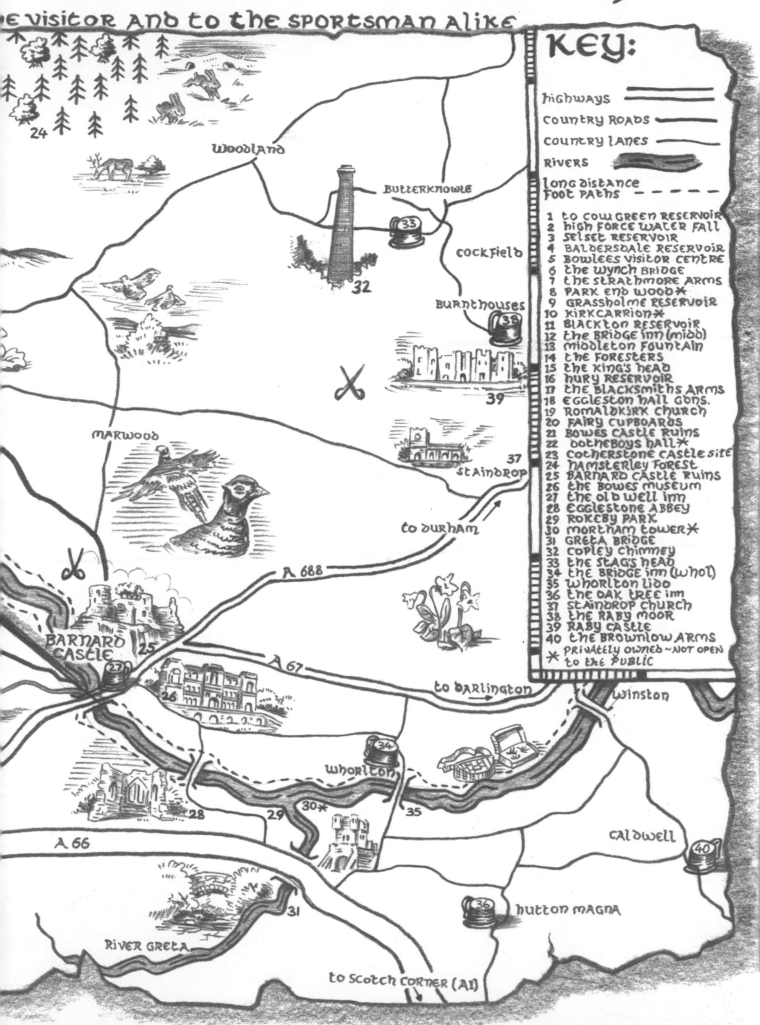

Woodland

Butterknowle
33

Cockfield

Burnthouses
38

32

39

Marwood

37
Staindrop

to Durham

A 688

BARNARD CASTLE
25
27

A 67

26

to Darlington

Winston

34

Whorlton

35

28 29 30*

Caldwell
40

A 66

36 **Hutton Magna**

31

RIVER GRETA

to Scotch Corner (A1)

KEY:

highways
country roads
country lanes
rivers
long distance
foot paths

1 to Cow Green Reservoir
2 High Force Water Fall
3 Selset Reservoir
4 Baldersdale Reservoir
5 Bowlees Visitor Centre
6 the Wynch Bridge
7 the Strathmore Arms
8 Park End Wood ✳
9 Grassholme Reservoir
10 Kirk Carrion ✳
11 Blackton Reservoir
12 the Bridge Inn (Midd)
13 Middleton Fountain
14 the Foresters
15 the King's Head
16 Hury Reservoir
17 the Blacksmiths Arms
18 Eggleston Hall Gdns.
19 Romaldkirk Church
20 Fairy Cupboards
21 Bowes Castle Ruins
22 Dotheboys Hall ✳
23 Cotherstone Castle Site
24 Hamsterley Forest
25 Barnard Castle Ruins
26 the Bowes Museum
27 the Old Well Inn
28 Egglestone Abbey
29 Rokeby Park
30 Mortham Tower ✳
31 Greta Bridge
32 Copley Chimney
33 the Stag's Head
34 the Bridge Inn (Whol)
35 Whorlton Lido
36 the Oak Tree Inn
37 Staindrop Church
38 the Raby Moor
39 Raby Castle
40 the Brownlow Arms
✳ privately owned ~ not open
   to the Public

24

A Teesdale Gazetteer:

(The information contained in this section was correct at the time of publication. However, visitors are urged to check that it is still valid and not to rely on telephone numbers, contacts, times and services remaining constant.)

The Northumbria Tourist Board.	0191 375 3000	Publishers of regional & special guides.
Durham County Council Tourism Department	0191 386 4411	Publishers of County & 'Walkabout Guides'.
Teesdale District Council Tourism Department	01833 690000	Publishers of local guides and listings.
Barnard Castle Tourist Information Centre	01833 690909	Helpful local source of information & help.
The Bowes Museum	01833 690606	World ranked museum. Small entry fee.
Bowlees Visitor Centre, near Middleton	01833 622292	Interpretive wildlife and history centre.
Eggleston Hall Gardens	01833 650378	Large walled gardens, small entry fee.
English Heritage for:	01833 638212	
Barnard Castle (ruins)		Small entry fee, substantial ruins remain.
Eggleston Abbey (ruins)		Entry free, glorious setting, worth visiting.
Bowes Castle (ruins)		Entry free, interesting village and church.
Forestry Commission for Hamsterly Forest	01388 488712	Activities, interpretive trails, well managed.
Killhope Lead Mining Centre (Weardale)	01388 537505	Excellent 'living' museum, small entry fee.
Raby Castle	01833 660202	Magnificent castle & deer park, entry fee.
Raby Estates for High Force (Northern Bank)	01833 622324	Small entry fee, glorious walk to the falls.
Rokeby Park	01833 637334	Outstanding setting. Opening restricted.
N.R.A./Environment Agency	01325 480849	Guardians of the environment.
Pollution Freephone	0800 807060	Please report all pollutions immediately.
Fishing Tackle and Permits from:		
R. Oliver, Wilkinsons, Barnard Castle	01833 631118	Knowledgeable advice & wide range of tackle.
J. Raine, Middleton-in-Teesdale	01833 640406	Local advice, more limited range of tackle.
Tees Riverflow Information	0891 154503	
Fishing Permits from:		
Raby Estate Office, Middleton	01833 640209	Office hours only, see above.
Northumbria Water Plc for reservoir fishing:	01833 650204/	Rainbow and Brown trout. Moderate charges
Cow Green, Selset, Grassholm,	0191 383 2222	for exceptional still water fishing, National License
Baldersdale, Blacton and Hury		fees are included in day permits.
Selset Sailing Club	01833 640504	Dinghy sailing and instruction. Seasonal.
	01833 621201	Phones not always manned, ask at T.I.C.
Balderhead Water Ski Club	01833 650310	Tow launches, 2 slaloms & jump. Seasonal.
	01748 824271	Phone not always manned, ask at T.I.C.
Grouse, Partridge and Pheasant Shooting from:		
The Raby Estates	01833 660360	Some of the very best organised and catered
H & W Sporting Estates	01207 529663	for shooting in the North of England.
Clay Pigeon Shooting, Teesdale Gun Club	01833 631118	Monday evening shoots. Annual competitions.
Canoeing, Four Seasons, Barnard Castle	01833 637829	International standard tuition, equipment hire.
River and Tees Barrage Slalom		
Cycle Hire, Barnard Castle	01833 690194	Cycles for all the family, moderate rates.

THE BLACKSMITH'S ARMS,
MICKLETON

Teesdale Sports Centre. Tennis, Swimming Etc.	01833 690400	Excellent modern indoor sports complex.
Barnard Castle Lawn Tennis Club	01833 637396	Several all-weather courts in attractive settings.
Barnard Castle Bowls Club	01833 627356	Good Green set in Bowes Museum grounds.
Barnard Castle Golf Club (18 Holes)	01833 638355	Flat topography, well equipped Club House.

Horse Riding centres at:

Lartington	01833 690118	Many bridleways and stretches of open country
Baldersdale,	01833 650474	set in fine and varied scenery. All abilities are
Hamsterly Forest	01388 767419	catered for from beginner to expert. Some
" "	01388 488328	provision for riders with disabilities.
Evenwood Gate	01388 833542	Indoor school, arena and dressage.

Ramblers, Barnard Castle Branch	01833 637825	Teesdale and Pennine Way Walks + 100's more

Training and Adventure Centres (both day and residential):

The Foresters, Middleton-in-Teesdale	01833 640836	Foresters offers full professional audio-visual
Kingsway, Middleton-in-Teesdale	01833 640881	training suite and small conference facilities.
Hudeway Centre, Middleton-in-Teesdale	01833 640012	Adventure centres cater for all ages, abilities
High Force Training Centre	01833 622302	and size of groups. Wide range of activities
Barnard Castle High Point Centre	01833 690118	available from trained, safety conscious staff.

Teesside International Airport, Darlington	01325 332811	Teesdale may be easily accessed from the A1(M)
Newcastle International Airport	0191 286 0966	or the M6 trunk roads and is linked to Europe by
Manchester International Airport	0161 489 3000	the Port of Tyne.
Darlington Railway Station	01325 355111	East Coast Main Line, express service.

A Simplified Countryside Code:

Please remember that, although the countryside appears to be tranquil and natural, it is also the 'factory floor' for farmers, foresters, gamekeepers and the like. Observing a few common sense rules will help to ensure that visitors will continue to be as welcome tomorrow as they are today:

*   Do not pollute still or moving waters. Report suspected pollutions on 0800 807060.

*   Do not start fires. Take particular care in dry conditions. Extinguish cigarettes with care.

*   Use gates and styles properly. Close all gates. Do not climb over dry stone walls and fences.

*   Keep dogs under adequate supervision. Be particularly careful if lambs are visible.

*   Take your litter back with you. Collect litter left by people less thoughtful than yourselves.

*   Stick to Public Rights of Way. The Trail Maps are rough guides only, please check routes at the time.

*   Please do not pick wild flowers, disturb wildlife or make unnecessary loud noise.

THE RABY MOOR INN,
BURNTHOUSES

AUTHOR'S NOTE.

Thanks to our sponsors Carlsberg-Tetley, and the kind help and encouragement of The Rural Development Commission. "Treats, Trails and Tavern Tales" has been 'distilled' and illustrated with you and your whole family in mind. Serving as a magic carpet, it will transport you, and those who are unable to make the actual physical journey to Teesdale, to share in its unique, unhurried and relaxing charm.

Ever mindful of Henry Burton's pointed sixteenth century criticism; "They lard their lean books with the fat of others", each separate fact, fancy and strand, which so many other authors and chroniclers have toiled previously to record, has been borrowed, enriched and woven together to create a colourful pattern for the amusement and pleasure of the reader.

This is a celebration of our remarkable valley, described as "England's Last Wilderness"; an environment where free spirits mingle with pure spirits; a magical land into which you are cordially invited to enter.